FAMILY
VACATIONS

THE DREYFUS FAMILY MONEY MANAGEMENT SERVICE

FAMILY VACATIONS:
More Fun for
Less Money

By FRANCES HUFF
with Darrell Huff

and the Editors of Dreyfus Publications

illustrated by John Huehnergarth

DREYFUS PUBLICATIONS LTD.　　NEW YORK

FRANCES HUFF qualified herself for the writing of this book (with her husband Darrell) by trying out in person all of the various family vacations she describes, and capped it all, on completion of the manuscript, by embarking on a tour of many months with her collaborator—but without any other family. She was her husband's collaborator on another book in this series, *How to Save on the Home You Want*.

THE DREYFUS FAMILY MONEY MANAGEMENT SERVICE

Jay Gold
VICE-PRESIDENT, EDITORIAL

Spero Yianilos
ASSISTANT EDITOR

Sandylee Williams
EDITORIAL ASSISTANT

John M. Hix
ART CONSULTANT

DREYFUS PUBLICATIONS LTD.

Jerome S. Hardy
PRESIDENT

Heinz E. Eller
EXECUTIVE VICE-PRESIDENT

Daniel Maclean
LEGAL DEPARTMENT

Sally J. Reich
Martin Stone
VICE-PRESIDENTS

Robert F. Dubuss
FINANCIAL ADVISOR

Arlene Armstrong
BUSINESS OFFICE

CONTENTS

6

A NOTE TO THE READER

This book, like its companion volumes in this series, has been planned to be as functional as it is informative. For that reason, the typographic design for the text specifies exceptionally wide margins. These are meant to be used for anything that will be helpful to you: for notetaking, reminders to yourself or even doing arithmetical calculations. The editors hope you will find the margins useful.

The stock for these books was selected in part because it can be written on equally well with pencil, or ballpoint or felt-tipped pen.

The colored rules you will find scattered throughout the book are used to emphasize salient portions of the text.

— THE EDITORS

CHAPTER I

At Home Away from Home

One summer Kathryn and Bob Fields and their three boys swapped their apartment in a San Francisco suburb for a ranch house in an historic and picturesque vineyard area fifty miles away, known as the Valley of the Moon.

Their three-weeks vacation cost them not one cent more than they would have spent at home during that period. Their house trade was made with some old friends who wanted to get away from valley heat and wine country scenery. For them, visiting city shops, museums and restaurants, in the cool fog that rolled thickly over San Francisco in August, was a welcome change.

Neither family bought anything new for this vacation. And neither toted along much except clothing. For mutual convenience each family used whatever food the other had left in the refrigerator. Instead of marring their vacation with conscientious housekeeping, the two wives agreed in advance that both would take it easy and each would clean up her own home upon return. The families solved the pet problem, that perennial vacation-time headache, by exchanging animal care, too.

The informal house-swap offers so many advantages that it is rapidly becoming an institution. Coast-to-coast and even international exchanges are almost as easy as next-door ones to arrange — and often far more enjoyable.

Thus one New York family spent ten days at Christmas in a tropical setting in the Caribbean, while the Caribbean family enjoyed its first Christmas with snow, living in the Manhattan brownstone apartment of the New Yorkers.

Organizations have sprung up to help arrange appropriate house-swaps of this sort; a partial listing can be found in the appendix.

Of course, house-swapping is not for everybody everytime. If the time or the place in which you want a house is rather rigidly fixed by circumstances or

House-swapping is an inexpensive way of vacationing
in a stimulatingly different environment. Example:
a house on a Caribbean isle for an apartment in New York City.

choice, you may not find anyone to trade with. Or the
demand for rentals in your home locality may be so
heavy that it's more profitable to rent out your residence and use part of the money to pay for one you
want elsewhere to vacation in.

This may be true abroad as well as here. In either
case, there are essentially two approaches.

The easy and safe way is by prearrangement. If your
goal is within the United States, this will probably
mean obtaining newspapers from the locality in question and answering "vacation rental" ads, or writing
to real-estate firms whose advertising indicates they
handle what you're after.

For a vacation residence abroad you may use the same method if you can obtain copies of English-language newspapers published in the areas, or if you can handle the language in question or have someone around who can help you. Vacationers' meccas like Rome, Paris, and Athens — not to mention London — have newspapers published in English.

For even more effortless arranging you can write to specialized rental agencies for lists and catalogs of thousands of houses all over the world that are available for short-term rentals.

The rich go vacationing too, often making it
possible for a non-rich family to rent a vacation home
impossibly — and gloriously — beyond their means.

These agencies list anything from a thatched-roof
Irish cottage or a Swiss mini-chateau to an Italian
palazzo. Some dwellings are sparsely furnished. Others are lavish and include the services of a maid,
gardener and cook.

If you've always wanted to live in, say, Paris this is
one way to do it. Rooms or apartments whose owners
are away on vacation can be had for about $200
a month (minimal rental, 2 weeks). You'll also be
required to put up one month's rent as a breakage
and cleaning deposit, refundable if the dwelling is
clean and there's no damage when you leave.

For house-swapping, some general principles apply
equally at home and abroad.

In any house exchange or short-term rental arrangement, it's essential to get the terms in writing. References should be exchanged. A bank reference is a good thing to get, too.

You'll need to have in writing a number of pesky details: Who pays for the utilities? Is there a phone? Who pays for it? Does the maid "come with the house"? Are you responsible for her salary? If you're bringing a pet, ask for permission. If you plan to leave pets of your own at home for renters to care for, be sure the other family is willing and able to feed and care for them properly.

If you are exchanging houses, consider a car exchange, too. It may be more convenient and less expensive to fly to the destination, leaving your own car for tenants to use and finding theirs ready for you in their garage.

Peculiarities and defects as well as assets

Be honest. List the peculiarities and defects as well as the assets of your own home when offering it. Expect — and ask for — the same in return. There just aren't many houses that don't have some problem — a fireplace that smokes, a basement that could flood in a storm, a dishwasher that leaks if you don't know how to close the door in a special way.

If you're of an economical, or a self-reliant, turn of

Save yourself a bundle by finding a vacation rental yourself,
thus eliminating the cost of an agent's commission.

mind you can save a great part of rental costs by
seeking out your own place, because cutting out the
middleman also cuts out about half the cost. This
system is especially appropriate if you don't have a
fixed goal, just an urge to live for a short time in some
general region. Then you're not at the mercy of the
real-estate market in one place; if what you want is
not quickly available in one town you can move on
at once to the next.

Though vacation house-renting is easier to manage in your own country, it is entirely feasible abroad. Language problems? These can be instructive even in English-speaking countries. A friendly woman from Auckland, New Zealand, once told us that the back-yards of her native city looked terrible "with all those hill hoists." Thus did we learn that we had a hill hoist in our own backyard at home for, seeing our bewilderment, she went on to explain that it was nothing more than the familiar, umbrella-type of clothesline.

True, language problems can cause at least temporary distress. For example, there's nothing like looking out a train window and seeing half of your vacationing family headed in the opposite direction on the wrong train — or were they on the right and you on the wrong?

That's what happened to us when our group accidentally got separated in a Swiss village and ended up in two moving trains, only one of which could be headed for our destination — the famed Matterhorn. Even the conductor on our train got a little panicky when he sized up the situation. Everybody was yelling — things like, "Stop! Stop! They're on the wrong train!" — in quite an assortment of languages.

We still don't know how it got straightened out, but apparently both conductors blew whistles and pulled cords. The trains stopped. Everybody cheered while we were reunited.

To Tahiti for peanut butter

Supermarket sleuthing in new places can be fun. In Tahiti once, our finds in a *service libre* — free service — store included such exotica as Skippy peanut butter, Minute Rice, Campbell's soups and Tang orange crystals as well as products from China, India, New Zealand and Australia. We continued to subsist largely on the local stuff: fresh coconut, mangoes and papaya, plentiful and cheap in contrast to the tinned foods from the US and elsewhere, which displayed dust on top of many cans — obviously they didn't move fast — and high prices.

Here's our own find-a-rental record during European vacations, at costs varying from about $1 a day to $200 a month for a family party of four to six:
• The French Riviera: We talked to two real-estate people in a village, looked at two houses and two

A little mix-up: one part of the family on a
train heading in one direction, another part on another
train heading in another direction, plus a language barrier.

apartments the first day, moved into a charming if inefficient tiny villa the second day later. Rented for one month, stayed two.

• Naples, Italy: We met an American Navy family at a campground, learned of a vacant, half-furnished apartment in their building, moved in the next day for a one-week stay.

• Palma de Mallorca, Spain: We found a large seafront mansion within an hour with the help of a real-estate firm specializing in rentals to foreigners. Moved in the next day for a month.

• Torremolinos, Spain: Arrived February 1, found a house near the sea within an hour through a rental agency, stayed two months.

• Black Forest, Germany: While camping, we met a girl from Wisconsin with a German husband, learned that their country house was vacant and rented it for a month at a price that was almost a gift.

A house in a storm

• Athens, Greece: We spent a day with real-estate people looking at stuffy flats, then took refuge from a momentary storm in a suburban restaurant. The proprietor pointed out a two-family house in the same block with the upstairs apartment available. Moving in the next day, we spent three pleasant months there.

• Copenhagen, Denmark: Through an agency specializing in summer houses, we rented a modernized, thatched-roof farm house on a pond for the one week we had open.

Before you commit yourself to rent a vacation-time house or to swap for one, you should consider the pro-and-con aspects. Here are the advantages:
• Travel can be exhausting, especially if the trip is an extended one, but staying put for a while is restful. There's no frequent packing, unpacking. Anytime you want a complete rest, you can have it when you have a suitable home.
• For large families especially, hotels and motels are expensive and confining.
• When there's a baby along, living in a house makes for comparatively easy care with no worries about other guests being disturbed by crying. Eating and food preparation are easier and the bedtime schedule can be fairly regular.
• An invalid or elderly person in the family group need not be excluded from this type of vacation. Their special needs can be met and activities can be geared to their capacities.
• Family pets needn't stay home or be put in a kennel.
• A parent with business obligations can keep in touch with his office and spend a portion of the day on business affairs without keeping others from sightseeing.
• Brief tutoring sessions can be worked in for children who have been taken out of school or are in need of additional schooling.
• You can cook at your vacation home when you wish, eat out when you choose. You're not tied to restaurant menus or mealtimes as you would be in a motel or hotel.
• You can have guests: people you meet who are on vacation, too, or friends from back home.

• You get to know a place better when you live in it.

• If you've chosen a vacation area with a climate or altitude different from your own, you'll have time to adjust. It requires several days for sea-level dwellers to adjust to the altitude of a mountain cabin.

And sometimes, by dint of staying in one place for a time, and being lucky, someone in your group might chance upon an incident that will live in memory.

It was a rainy night in Monaco, a few miles from where we were living in our rented house on the French Riviera. Kay and Carolyn, our teenage daughters, had finally persuaded us to let them make a visit with a pair of male contemporaries to the famous

A nice thing about having a home as home base on a
family junket is that it's easy for everyone to go his own way.

Monte Carlo Casino. No luck. A firm doorman turned them away when he found they were under 21. Instead of joining international society, the girls found themselves waiting under a drippy hotel marquee while their escorts sought return transportation.

The case of the handsome stranger

At that moment three smartly dressed adults crossed from the casino and entered the lobby door, paying no attention to our two daughters — or so the girls thought. A few minutes later the tallest, a handsome, graying man returned.

In a clipped British accent he asked, "Do you girls need any help? I must say, though, yours are the two most cheerful faces I've seen all evening."

"I guess not," said Kay. "We'd hoped to see the inside of the casino, but we're not old enough. They won't let us in even to take a look."

The man smiled sympathetically. "Oh, that's too bad. A few minutes ago I could have arranged it. Mr. Onassis was with me and he might have been able to help."

When the girls reached home and told their story the family verdict was that the fellow was just an imaginative name-dropper and probably up to no good. But the next day we picked up a local newspaper and saw an airport photograph of Cary Grant and Aristotle Onassis — "Visitors to Monte Carlo."

The handsome, thoughtful stranger had escaped recognition by the girls, though they were fans of his, because of his unexpected British accent. He hadn't been exaggerating about friendship with the then-owner of the casino, just the man who could have helped the girls see the place.

(The girls forced the rest of us to agree that a man is not a name-dropper if he neglects to mention his own when it has the glamour of Cary Grant, then at the peak of his movie-star career, attached to it.)

Whether or not Cary Grant has a place in your pantheon of movie stars, you will probably acknowledge that a house-for-vacation has its plusses. Of course, it also has minuses. Here are some of them:

• It's easy to get lazy when you're too comfortable. You may not do as much sightseeing or absorb other pleasures of travel as you would if you thought you were going to move on each day.

• Daily routine will still be there, particularly, as a rule for the wife: meals to get, beds to make, laundry to do.

• You have responsibility for your vacation home. If something breaks down or is damaged, you'll have to fix it or get a repairman.

• If you're swapping houses with friends, you run the risk of damaging that friendship. Carelessness, or an accident, or loss of a friend's possessions can lead to trouble.

• A change to another house may not be change enough. You might benefit more from a vacation completely different from the rest of your year.

So much for the pros and cons of swapping or renting houses for a vacation. You can achieve much the same thing, except it's not the same thing, by renting a motor home.

An unusually comfortable, but very different, vacation in a home on wheels might be right for you. Motor homes come with all kinds of comforts: TV, stereo, shag carpeting, tub with hot shower.

You can drive and park one almost as easily as a family car. You can live in it at a park, a camp, or parked in a friend's driveway while you visit. You can take it into the wilderness, to a beach, or you can put it aboard a ferry and take it to an island or to Alaska.

Motor homes are available from U-Haul, rental-car agencies, and private owners. If you fly in, Avis or Hertz can have one waiting for you at the airport. You can rent one for a weekend or a month. You can often arrange to apply rental cost to purchase price if you discover you can't live without it.

Motor home rentals can be expensive — often a couple of hundred dollars a week in the busy season. But for a large family the cost of a motor home may not be out of line. For a small family economy may suggest sharing the trip with another small family.

Families who buy motor homes often recoup part of the cost by renting to others. Watch for offerings in the newspapers. Or run your own want-ad.

Be warned, though: quite a few families have become so enamored of a vehicular house while vacationing that they have taken up permanent residence in it.

CHAPTER II

Abroad
at Home,
and Vice Versa

For a memorable and significant vacation experience you can visit a foreign country without leaving your own country. The US has hundreds of communities where people speak their native (foreign) tongues, cook and eat national and ethnic foods, dress and play the way their forebears did in other lands — and this not too far from where you live.

Some have a foreign flavor year-round. Others turn foreign for a day or a week once a year when the inhabitants put on a festival to re-create briefly their foreign past.

Have you had time lately to take a trip to the Sahara desert? Few ever see this distant scene, but there's a region a few miles west of Yuma, Arizona, where mountainous sand dunes often provide a convincing movie location for Bedouins, sheiks, and camels. If camels are absent while you're visiting, you can find them at Virginia City, Nevada, where camel races (ostrich, too) take place annually in early September. And there may still be wild camels roaming in arid spots of that state where some were turned loose long ago. (Miners imported them in 1860 to haul supplies. When the desert beasts proved ill-adapted to mining life some were abandoned to fend for themselves, and they obviously did just that.)

If camels aren't exotic enough for you, try a trip to the moon. At Craters of the Moon National Monument in Idaho, at Lassen National Park in northern California, and at the volcanic plains and caves of California's Lava Beds National Monument (300 volcanic caves) you'll encounter convincing facsimiles of barren lunar landscape. Our astronauts did some of their training in these places.

For a "moon trip" wear heavy-soled shoes. Carry water if you go in summer. Developed camp areas nearby have facilities for stopovers.

To sample the rain forest of the Amazon without going to South America, head for Olympic National

Park in northern Washington, where some spots receive several hundred inches of rain a year. It's authentic rain forest: moss-covered trees, giant ferns, decayed "nurse" logs with new trees growing from them, rain-forest animals, and — in developed areas — camping spots with ranger-guides to take you on a trek through the forest. It will probably rain, so be prepared. Carry mosquito repellent.

Does "rain forest" say "South America" to you? It needn't, for you can find one to explore in the US too.
Locale: a national park in the Pacific Northwest.

You can cram several foreign countries into just one visit to a big city. New York, Chicago, Los Angeles, San Francisco, New Orleans, and some smaller cities have foreign enclaves.

San Francisco's Golden Gate Park has an authentic Japanese tea garden. You can see a Japanese shrine, an arched bridge over a stream, Oriental flowers, and then have tea and rice cakes served by a waitress in a kimono. At dinnertime go to a Japanese restaurant near the Wharf, take off your shoes and sit on a floor mat at a low table where you will be served food prepared at the table while you watch.

Drumming in the new year

Also in the same city, a 6-block Chinatown near Grant Street, with theaters, imported goods of all kinds and herbs and unusual vegetables in grocery stores, a joss house temple. Even the Pacific Telephone Company building is an example of Chinese architecture. Tour a Chinese fortune cookie factory. If you make your San Francisco visit in February, you can celebrate New Year's with the Chinese — firecrackers, incessant drumming, a dragon parade.

Vacationing in New York City, try Mulberry Street for Italian atmosphere, Mott Street for Chinese. In New Orleans Le Vieux Carré is a district out of old France. Go to the northeast corner of the US and cross (cheating a little on the premise of this chapter) to Quebec City where the shop signs, food, and people are more French than in France.

On our other coast, you can board a ferry at Port Angeles, Wash., with your car and cross (cheating a little more) to Victoria, British Columbia. There you'll experience England as it was years ago, a bit old fashioned and surrounded by British accents.

Shops sell British biscuits (crackers to you) tea, bone china, woolens and cashmere, and sweets (we call it candy). You can "take tea" at the famous old Empress Hotel. On the streets you'll see flower baskets of blue lobelia, pink geranium, and orange nasturtiums swinging from lamp posts — reminders of British gardening expertise. There's lawn tennis, there are gentlemen in white shirts and slacks bowling on the green, and horse-carriage rides that are not just for tourists; local residents use them, too.

As an American family of six visiting Victoria we experienced some of this British hospitality and charm when our loaded station wagon had a flat tire smack in front of city hall. Hesitantly we pulled out of heavy traffic into a zone clearly marked *Reserved for the Mayor.*

Before we could touch our tire a regal white-haired lady, wearing a flowered toque (a hat in the style favored by Queen Mary in the '20s) emerged from the building and announced: "Welcome to Victoria. I am a member of the council. I saw your distress. You need not worry. Stay in this parking place as long as necessary."

Here are more abroad-at-home towns:

Switzerland is represented by New Glarus, Wisconsin. This town of 1,400 Swiss immigrants, 30 miles from Madison, offers cheese factories, a picturesque countryside with cows wearing Swiss bells, yodeling concerts, model dairy farms. William Tell Festival is the first week in September.

Denmark is in California at Solvang, a few miles north of Santa Barbara. It was founded in 1911 by Danes. Here are Danish signposts, architecture, imitation stork nests on roofs, Danish-made dishes, silver and fabrics. You can eat Danish coffee-cake called *kringler* or dine on Danish-style hamburgers called *frikadeller*. There's a festival with folk dancing in mid-September.

Dutch clothes, food, music, beach grass

For Dutch tulips you can make the festival at — where else? — Holland, Michigan, in the spring. All year here the atmosphere is Dutch. So are the costumes, music, food, and glimpses of sand dunes with sea grass, all amazingly the way it is along the (real) Dutch coast.

Drive through Lancaster County in Pennsylvania, where "Pennsylvania Dutch" towns and countryside

The word "tulips" equals Holland, right? Right:
but in this case it's Holland, Michigan.

reproduce German towns and countryside. Potato pancakes, *Sauerbraten*, and *Wiener Schnitzel* are served in restaurants. You'll see hex signs displayed on barns and find other old customs preserved.

The soft, rolling, green hills and stark coal-mining atmosphere around Wilkes Barre, Pa., simulate the countryside of Wales in the United Kingdom.

Spain? Try Albuquerque, New Mexico, for Spanish-plus-Indian atmosphere, Spanish-American food, un-usual craft work. Or cross the border (cheating a little again) to Mexico. Take the 1,200 mile road from Tijuana to Cabo San Lucas in Baja California, but make sure you're driving a rugged car and carrying plenty of supplies and water. This is arid country, where you're on your own much of the way, though Mexican people are helpful and friendly.

For the Spain of Andalusia go to Santa Barbara, California, especially during the so-called Spanish Days in August, when there are parades and authentic Old-Spain costumes to be seen.

Welcome to the winery

For France, tour the Sonoma and Napa valleys, 50 miles north of San Francisco, to see French vineyard country, particularly beautiful in the fall. Seek out the old stone-building wineries. You will be welcomed.

In or close to the US you will best find Scotland in Nova Scotia, where the climate and the moors mimic the original. There's a little France here, too, in Louis-bourg, only a fishing village now, but once a French stronghold in the New World.

One-time Bohemia and Moravia, since World War I part of Czechoslovakia, have a counterpart in northeast Iowa, at Spillville, where the famed Czech composer Anton Dvořák wrote the New World Symphony and played the organ for Mass at St. Wenceslaus, a church that invokes images of many in Bohemia.

All over our country you'll discover larger regions as well as towns resembling their counterparts abroad. The Grand Tetons of Wyoming could be Swiss Alps. Date palms and dunes of Arizona could be in North Africa. Minnesota has a Swedish population and atmosphere. The coast of the Big Sur, 25 miles south of Monterey in California, could be the Grand Corniche of the Riviera in France, with that rare kind of terrain where mountains meet sea — abruptly. And the London Bridge at Lake Havasu City, Arizona, 235 miles east of Los Angeles, really *is* London Bridge, dismantled and transported there from England, stone by stone.

Foreign-language farms

An especially enjoyable way to gain a foreign experience without going far from home is to look for a farm that caters to speakers of the language whose country you are interested in. (See the chapter on farm and ranch vacations.) There, fresh from their own countries, you can meet speakers of Spanish, Swedish, Italian, Hebrew, Portuguese, Norwegian, Polish, Danish, German, Dutch, French — even Finnish, Hungarian, Icelandic, Korean, Esthonian.

For years when your taste for foreign travel is strong but the opportunity is lacking, an abroad-at-home vacation can be a fine substitute and introduction to the real thing. A family already introduced to a new language, to new foods, and to people who live differently, is inoculated against the fear of cultural shock that keeps many Americans from venturing far from their own borders.

CHAPTER III

Family Vacations Custom-Made

Cast: Mr. and Mrs. James Parker.
   Two Parker teenagers (difficult).
   Two younger Parkers, age 6 and 8, given to tem-
     peramental outbursts at the onset of boredom.
Time elapsed: one month.
Place: Mexico.
Script: riding burros and horses; watching a wood-
en saddle being carved, then bargaining to buy it;
attending a bullfight; collecting amethyst and obsid-
ian for a rock collection; visiting churches (lost track
of the count) and art museums (ditto); learning how
to make tortillas; shopping for rugs and fabrics; touring food markets; making the rounds of cafes to
tape-record mariachi music; collecting Mexican folk-

music records; dining and sleeping in a castle; touring an underground cemetery; exploring Aztec ruins and "helping" archaeologists at a dig; taking pictures for a photographic study of social conditions; photographing geologic formations and the effects of erosion; touring housing projects; learning how to prepare turkey mole.

And on and on.

Doing violence to the family's social fabric

Can you picture all these things done by all six Parkers so disparate in age, taste, interests, physical fitness, etc., without violence done to the family social fabric? Of course you can't.

You can pretty well measure the success of a family vacation by the extent to which each member succeeds in doing his own thing — which may be quite different from anyone else's. The family that stays together steadily on a long vacation may become merely the family that is bored together.

No one member of the Parker family did all the things listed above or would want to. Frequently the older two children went off from the others, alone or together. Sometimes the parents took the younger two on side trips, but often left them in care of a dude-

No family should overdo the togetherness bit just
because all the members are vacationing together.

ranch wrangler to ride burros. The parents went out in the evening several times while one of the teenagers did a baby-sitting stint. When the older four found a late-evening adventure to share, the younger two stayed with a Mexican baby-sitter — and in one way or another picked up quite a bit more Spanish than their elders did.

Opportunities to keep togetherness from getting sticky during vacations will arise regularly — and should be grasped.

On the first leg of a trip to Australia and New Zealand our Qantas Airways steward rushed to apologize for seating that separated man and wife. Though not by much actually — we were only an aisle apart. He'd persuade somebody to change, he promised, and have us together "in a jiff."

We both said, "No."

The rewards of separation

We had already learned there is profit in a degree of separateness. One of us was already deep in conversation with her seatmate, a lady returning to Auckland who was soon to extend an invitation to come for tea and an introduction to New Zealand upon our arrival, scheduled for a few weeks later.

Conversation in the seats on the other side of the aisle was equally pleasant and productive. There the other of us was learning details of places to visit and things to do in India later on from an Aussie who had worked there for his government's foreign department for two years.

There's another bonus available to couples, and sometimes whole families, who arrange for separate seats when making travel reservations. Each person may be able to obtain a seat on the window side and thus actually see something outside the vehicle.

Just to get your thinking launched, here is a suggested list of specialized vacation activities. Consider the interests and ages of the members of your own family. There's no real reason to force everyone to participate in identical experiences. Some might be enjoyed by the whole family together or by just one or two members.

• Take a trip into history.

Visit a restored American city of the past (Williamsburg, Va. is the best known); try out pioneering (there's an outfit that runs covered-wagon tours, jolting but authentic); pan for gold; tour museums displaying artifacts from homes, shops, and schools of the past; see people making wooden casks, carving figureheads for ships, sewing sails; browse in a costume museum; visit an historic commune; do some square dancing; record and collect country music; tour Revolutionary or Civil War battle areas.

• For the geology buff.

Examine an earthquake fault (San Andreas in California is the most evident); photograph and identify rock formations; visit a volcanic cinder cone (Mt. Lassen in northern California); tour an oil field in Texas; visit a copper mine, an iron ore site, a coal mine; see an old assaying office (Virginia City, Nevada); study gold mining equipment near Sutter Creek, California; explore red sandstone sculpture in southern Utah and northern Arizona; explore a lava bridge and ice cave rift, 800 feet deep, at Great Rift National Monument, Idaho.

• Be an archaeologist.

Find your own dig (an old campsite, dump, or ruin) but get permission before digging on private property; explore an Indian pueblo in the Southwest; make a photo series of your dig; visit the old iron works at Saugus, Massachusetts (originally discovered by an untrained amateur archaeologist); explore a ghost town.

• Are you an artist?

Tour private and public galleries; look for stores selling art supplies; take along a sketch pad for an on-the-scene trip diary; take 35 mm or Polaroid shots to be used later as models for painting; visit a county or state fair to see what artists of the region are producing.

• Interested in sewing and clothing design?

Window-shop and browse through fabric stores; go to boutiques and look for new ideas; visit a costume museum (that's where many top designers get their ideas); watch for flea-market and rummage sales (often a source of fabrics for quilts or rugs); look for unusual buttons and braid (try antique and second-hand stores for these items, too); study folk design (Mexico, Indian country, ethnic areas throughout the US).

• Antique hunting.

Check a local phone book to get addresses of auction houses and antique shops; ask about flea markets; check with the local librarian on the location of historical houses exhibiting antiques; browse through second-hand stores.

If art is one of your things, use the opportunity provided by a vacation to visit an art museum new to you, and maybe copy a painting.

• A gourmet vacation.

Seek out restaurants with ethnic menus; stop at food stands in rural areas and try the specialties; visit a farm or factory producing unusual foods (Spice Island Company in San Francisco offers regular tours); collect interesting foods that are sold where they're processed (maple syrup in Vermont, pecan pralines in Louisiana, cheese in Wisconsin); collect cookbooks; see if there's a regional food festival (pancake day, watermelon-eating contest, pumpkin show, grape festival).

• For sports.

Check newspaper and local sports organizations for coming events; try the local sporting-goods stores; ask for guest or vacation-play privileges at a golf or tennis club (you'll usually be made welcome, probably at a small charge, almost anywhere in the world; bring along your membership card if you belong to a club at home); visit a sports-car center, a marina.

• For music.

Make the rounds of record shops to listen and collect; check the newspaper and watch for posters announcing musical events; bring your tape recorder and make a sound diary of your vacation, including street sounds.

• For architecture buffs.

Tour a town on foot, observing architectural styles; call or stop at an architect's office for clues to unusual or historic homes; ask at the local library about the area's housing history and interesting public buildings; check the classifieds (Saturday and Sunday issues are best) for "open houses" you can drop in on; take a city bus tour (most of them include architectural highspots).

• Crafts.

Check at the craft shops, which can clue you in on local craftsmen and where they work; visit a sculpture or pottery exhibit; ask if there's a craft class you can observe; collect books on your craft; take photos of other people's work; inquire if there's a local factory turning out handmade materials or unusual objects (ties, dresses, quilts, pottery).

Travel nourishes the inquisitiveness of an architecture
buff, who will never find any one place as diverse
in housing styles as the illustrator provides here.

• Photography.

Make a photo-diary of your trip; ask the local
camera store about local photography exhibits; check
magazine stands and bookstores for photographic
publications of the area.

We've just run through a sampling of ways to
make a family vacation meaningful — and fun
for everybody, but not necessarily the same for
everybody all the time. The trick, as noted
earlier, is to let everybody, as far as possible,
do his or her own thing.

CHAPTER IV

Mostly for Women: About Clothes, Luggage and Pickpockets

"Pack a black cashmere cardigan. You'll need it when you go camping and when you go to the opera."

This piece of vacation advice for women comes from one of the shrewdest travelers we know, one Madge Evans who, with her husband and four children, would rate high on anyone's list of best-dressed voyagers.

The Evanses have camped widely in the US, Mexico, and Europe.

Madge explains, "A cashmere sweater is great with slacks or skirt. It rolls up to fit into a large purse or pocket. It washes beautifully in cold water. It's a perfect foot warmer in a sleeping bag. It doubles as a pillow on an airplane or train. I dressed mine up with a couple of jeweled clips and threw it over my shoulders the night we saw *Don Giovanni* at the Vienna State Opera House."

Madge's sweater meets all these specifications for any item in a successful travel wardrobe:

1. Each garment should adapt to several occasions.
2. It should mix or match with other garments.
3. It should not wrinkle or show soil.
4. It should be conservative enough to avoid drawing unwelcome attention to you.
5. It should pass these use tests.

Wear it before you take it along, testing it for comfort and appearance. Go even further with shoes; give them a good breaking-in.

Garments that scratch, tug, pull or are difficult to put on and take off produce irritable travelers. Tight shoes make blisters, especially in hot weather when feet tend to swell.

Eliminate garments that are not washable. Dry cleaning is slow and unreliable for people on the move. Do-it-yourself dry cleaning machines are efficient, but beware.

After cleaning, heavy garments — and especially sleeping bags — must be thoroughly aired before use. People have died because they slept in bags or blankets too soon after cleaning.

Leave your iron at home and take along nothing that calls for its use. Garments will drip-dry quickly if excess water is blotted out with a sponge a few times during the drip period. Fabric can be smoothed with your hands while it's damp.

Plastic blow-up hangers promote fast and smooth drying. There's one kind that's shaped like a sweater and is great for shirts and blouses. (We've seen it at big department stores as well as in cosmetic departments of drugstores, for $1.)

A couple of weeks before departure, pack tightly into a suitcase all the main garments

A black cashmere sweater is fine with slacks, hot dogs and a campfire, and just as good with a long skirt, pearls, a bit of a haughty manner and an opera.

you're considering for the trip. Then take them out a few days later to make sure they're presentable after a quick shakeout.

For any trip during which varied temperatures may be met and luggage weight is a problem, adopt the layer system. A blouse plus a sleeveless slipover sweater plus a cardigan is a great cold weather assortment for a woman; on a warmer day she simply removes the cardigan and perhaps the slipover, too. A man who has a thin, cool shirt, a sweater, and a lightweight jacket can combine them to fit almost any temperature and weather condition.

A sleeveless dress becomes a warm jumper when worn with a blouse. Sweat suits (cotton-plus-acrylic doesn't wrinkle, dries faster than all-cotton) for women, men, and children (available through mail-order) look good for jogging or for informal shopping in a resort area, can become pajamas on a chilly night. Tights plus a T-shirt are a good combo, too. Zippered turtle-neck shirts or sweaters go up or down with the thermometer. Two pairs of thin socks are better than one pair of thick socks.

For an attractive wardrobe of minimum weight it's essential to coordinate colors. Basic dark blue or brown is good. Beware white — it will soil in a suitcase.

Get your color lift from such small accessories as scarves, ties, jewelry, belts (fun to shop for and bring home as souvenirs, too). If all your hosiery is one shade, a single snag or run won't wreck a whole pair. Choose a neutral color that will look good with everything.

Good clothing choices include: culottes (more acceptable than shorts and more comfortable); wrap-around skirts; zoris for beach or shower wear; a beret or foldup rain hat; a belt with concealed, zipped money compartment; a bandanna handkerchief; almost weightless nylon poncho that folds to pocket or purse size; non-run tights instead of pantyhose.

Shampoo for the laundry

Among take-alongs worth considering: a metal-bristled brush to clean mud or spots from suede shoes, which are a better choice than smooth leather for staying presentable; sealed individual envelopes of cleaning fluid (from drugstores) or a Spot Stick to remove stains; a tube of mild shampoo instead of slippery, hard-to-transport bar soap for hand washing; a laundry bag to keep soiled garments in one place, ready for a quick laundromat stop; marking pens in different colors for labeling individual garments or possessions; a stretch clothesline; tiny clothespins; a few huge baby-blanket pins (indispensable for improvising bedding and laundry arrangements); penlight or disposable flashlight for each traveler; folding umbrella to fit a purse (choose one in white, or ivory, as we did, and it will be a useful sun umbrella, too, as ours were on the black sand beach of Tahiti, where the dark surface increases the temperature, or the high-fog beaches of California, where skin is easily burned raw-red through the bright fog cover); colored sponge cloths, one color for each person and one for the dishes (they're better than washcloths because they won't mildew, can be boiled, can serve as towels, too); short-handled travel toothbrushes, or regular brushes with handles cut short (an old toothbrush makes a good cuff and collar scrubber.)

The last time we took a trip to a warm climate we thought we'd solved the nightly sock, pantie and shorts washing by buying those little packets of plastic capsules, each one of which contains enough detergent for a basin of water. But we found they became a gooey mess when the temperature climbed into the 90s. Ours melted into one big gob. So we've gone back to reliable bar soap.

Think of the temperatures, too, when you're getting prescriptions from your doctor. Some medications come in capsules similar to those in which we bought the treacherous detergent granules. It would be even more serious should a needed prescription melt into one sticky unusable dose, fit only for the garbage can.

If you covet the comfort and lightness of down sleeping bags but not their cost, you can save one-third to one-half the store price with sew-it-yourself

The authors say they have done well with a do-it-yourself
sewing kit for a sleeping bag — but you need patience.

kits. (See appendix for list of catalog houses.) Also
available for the home seamstress with patience for
detail and the ability to follow instructions are kits for
lightweight nylon tents, ponchos, and accessory bags.

We got first-rate results, using only a portable
sewing machine, making a man's down jacket, an
Arctic-weight sleeping bag, and a 2-man tent. They're
all good projects for long winter evenings, but nothing
to tackle if your time is short or your patience thin.

"Take no more luggage than you can carry in your
own two hands and be prepared to do it at a dead run
when you make that 200-yard dash to catch the next
plane or train," advises one seasoned traveler. He
knows that trunks and matched sets of luggage are as
obsolete as the porters and bellboys who used to
carry them.

If you're going to carry your luggage much, bags
should be lightweight above all. Some stores have
scales for comparison weighing. Choose waterproof

or at least water-repellent canvas, nylon fabric, or soft vinyl.

A bag is only as good as the thread it's stitched with: so ask if that's nylon or dacron thread, rather than cotton. Look for double-stitching and bar-tacking at stress points. The best zippers are the industrial-size plastic type that won't stick or snag. Some bags come with double zippers for easy access to both ends of the case. If one zipper breaks, the other serves as a spare.

Navy or army duffle bags are inexpensive, sturdy enough for soft gear, can double as pillows or child's bed in a car, stow away easily at home. Combination locks are better than key locks. Look for a strong tag or built-in-tag on the handle of a bag. Choose a visible color or distinctive fabric type that can be easily identified in a sea of luggage. You can personalize your luggage with a waterproof colored marking pen or bright tape. Look for wear-saving metal studs on the bag's bottom.

Is there an extra strap for over-the-shoulder carrying? Are the handles easy to grip? Are they riveted, not just single stitched? Are there several compartments to separate shoes and accessories? Is the lining made of waterproof material that will wipe clean?

If you must take more than you can lift, consider suitcases with built-in wheels, from $20 to $100, or get a combination of four wheels plus a canelike attach-ment to strap on to your present suitcase, around $11. Or buy a set of wheels to strap onto your bags.

• Take along a flat-folding lightweight bag inside your regular suitcase to bring back souvenirs and other overflow.

• Take a fliptop, or zippered, insulated diaper bag, sold in baby departments, for toting baby food, cold drinks, or sandwiches.

• Ziplock plastic bags, sold in rolls at grocery stores, seal to keep damp or spillables separated from clothing.

• Buy an ordinary dog leash or two, the kind with a snaplock on one end, to use if a suitcase handle breaks, a zipper jams, or you want to convert a hand-carry bag to an over-the-shoulder type. A dog leash snaps to a toddler's belt for temporary restraint in busy or dangerous areas.

Your bag will be stronger and the contents won't spill or crush if it's tightly packed. Put heavy items at the bottom, crushables on top of uncrushables. Tuck small items around the edges and in shoes. Coil belts around the inside perimeter of the bag. Padding gar-ment sleeves and shoulders with tissue lessens wrin-kling. Prevent soiling where it can hurt by turning light or white garments inside out.

Avoid courting embarrassment

Pack with care and double-check that all hatches are battened — or you're courting embarrassment. This truism was demonstrated to us while we were driving the family station wagon, with a little teardrop trailer attached, on an especially rough stretch of Mexican highway.

We'd forgotten to lock the trailer door and it only took one big pothole to pop open the door and spill our bright green homemade portable toilet right in the middle of the road.

We were a real traffic-stopper while scrambling around to collect what was now only kindling for our evening campfire.

Valuable jewelry is better left at home. Carry your travelers checks, necessary papers, and keys in a purse with a zippered compartment. A man's wallet should be put in his coat breast pocket, not in his trousers back pocket.

Fool pickpockets and prevent careless loss by sealing pockets with a sewn-in strip of Velcro, sold by the inch in fabric shops. Velcro is a two-part tape, strips of which adhere to themselves to make a fastening almost as tight as a zipper. It makes no bulge when sewn into a pocket, emits a scratchy noise if someone tries to pry it open stealthily.

Velcro works well on coat pockets too. We loss-proofed all our open pockets with Velcro after the male half of this writing team lost his passport out of a jacket thrown over a shoulder on a beach walk near Athens.

Make a last-minute packing check to be sure you've put in any of these miscellaneous handy-dandies you may need: shower cap; magnifying glass; folding plastic cup; packets of shoe shine, nail polish, hand and face clean-up tissues; sewing kit with needles threaded in assorted colors; a few buttons.

Also, an expense record diary, which will provide a permanent record of more than just the financial details of a trip if the record-keeper itemizes expenses, including names of places, types of purchases and the exact amounts spent each day.

CHAPTER V

Currency: Other Peoples' and Yours

Most of this book addresses itself to ways you can get the most for your money while vacationing — in short, to enjoy yourself without financial strain. This chapter will zero in not on how you spend your dollars but on how to have them available when and where you want them with the least effort and at the least cost.

Travelers checks should be your basic money. The $1 per $100 you generally pay as a fee when buying them is cheap insurance against loss. Any of the many kinds issued by banks will be accepted most places — and sometimes you can get these without paying a fee — but if you're going very far afield you just might

be happier if you stick to the well-known names: American Express, First National City, Cook and others. (If you're traveling abroad, particularly anywhere many Britons go, Thomas Cook checks may be particularly suitable. The Cook fee is one-fourth less and the name is well known worldwide.)

For use within your own country you'll probably want your checks mostly in small denominations, $10 being the smallest issued. Then you need never risk loss of much cash.

For foreign travel, get mostly larger denominations of travelers checks. You'll usually be exchanging checks for a fairly large amount of cash each time in order to avoid the poorer-than-bank rates of exchange beloved of restaurateurs and innkeepers and — worst of all — gas station operators on Germany's Autobahns.

Letters of credit, whereby an American bank extends you credit to a specified amount, to be drawn in cash at its correspondent banks abroad and which were once the traditional money tool of the traveler, are pretty much out of date. Using them too often means finding the right bank at an inconvenient hour and place. Even so, if your trip is a long or involved one, take the time to learn if your own bank can figure out how this kind of guarantee can be useful to you.

A bank check is probably the simplest and least expensive way to have funds sent to you while you are away. Also called a cashier's check, it may cost your account only 25 cents, perhaps plus postage, even when quite a large sum is involved.

If your travel is outside the US, this kind of check is more reliable than the more costly foreign draft that your bank may prefer to use.

The fondness of banks for foreign drafts is exceeded only by the distaste that travelers soon develop for them as a means of obtaining money. The gimmick is that one copy must reach you and one must reach a bank, offering double opportunity for something to go wrong.

The trouble with bank drafts

This is more than theory. Our whole traveling family of six was held up over a weekend in Amsterdam once, awaiting the delayed arrival of the bank's copy. The next time we wrote for funds, we underlined *cashier's check* three times — and our bank again sent a draft. We were in Copenhagen that time; by the time the bank there conceded that since their copy hadn't arrived after three days "it probably went to Stockholm," we were embarrassingly late for a birthday party at the home of Danish relatives in the north of Jutland.

Years later we went through similar agony with another bank draft (once again, not our choice). This happened in Tahiti. After a couple of hours of standing in lines and running about town in tropical heat, we gave that one up entirely, although we were constantly assured by the combined forces of American Express and the Banque de l'Indochine that the thing was cashable if we'd just wait long enough. We mailed that piece of paper back to our bank at home to be put back into our account. There it could be drawn upon far more readily by use of a simple personal check backed by an American Express credit card.

Don't let costs overwhelm your vacation.

Some banks will not issue cashier's checks to be sent abroad. So make your arrangements before you leave home if you have plans to use them in another country. Also try to verify that they will be signed by a bank officer whose signature is on the international list found in banks worldwide. Otherwise you could have trouble getting your money in, say, Singapore or Papeete.

Although it's risky to carry much cash when on the move, it can be highly inconvenient to arrive anywhere with no local currency. It's best to obtain at least a small sum of cash of the country you're going to before you get there.

This is primarily to tide you over your first small expenditures — tips at point of entry or first hotel, perhaps an initial cab ride.

There's another reason — the opportunity it gives you to examine the strange currency and learn what each piece is worth. (Memorize the value of coins and paper money by look *and* feel — size, or weight, or color or roughened edges.) Do that and you'll avoid the unnerving experience of an Australian we met on a Pacific island.

He'd flown in the night before and upon arriving at his hotel had handed over to the hotel-bus driver the requested 200 francs. This is not an especially shocking fare in the ordinary way of things, since the franc used in French Polynesia is worth only a little more than one American cent.

But the Aussie had somehow stocked up with French, not Polynesian, francs before leaving home and he awakened next morning with the realization that he'd handed over the equivalent of nearly $40 for a ride of a few miles.

Police intervention led the driver to return the excess after a day or two of stalling. "You could hardly blame the fellow, could you?" the Aussie summed up. "I pushed temptation right into his face without warning."

Free credit cards — the kind you don't pay a fee for — are an economical means of spending money without carrying it. There are some so widely acceptable all over the US that they can make carrying specialized cards (gasoline or air-travel, for example) unnecessary. And you may prefer to arrive home to face one big bill rather than a host of little ones from many suppliers of transportation and gas.

Banks commonly issue various kinds of courtesy, check-cashing, and check-guarantee cards, to preferred customers or people who think to ask for them. We have found that thousands of miles from home one of these free bits of pasteboard can mean the difference between prompt check honoring and a firm No. Ask your banker.

Credit cards you pay for can be an expensive luxury, particularly if they lead you into luxury purchases or a more costly dinner than you really wanted. But they do save trouble, confer status . . . perhaps — and help with bookkeeping. This last is really important if your trip has some business connection that may permit income-tax savings.

At first, interest-free — and then, 18%

One drawback to this system of money handling if yours is a long trip is that bills may arrive at home and remain unpaid unless you have someone there who can handle them for you. One way around this is to keep at least approximate track of amounts you charge, then send a check about the time you know the month's bill will be due.

Most uses of a credit card actually amount to an interest-free loan for a period of a couple weeks up to nearly two months. Then what you owe suddenly converts itself into a rather costly loan, most usually at 18% interest per year, unless you pay the full amount before the interest calculation begins.

To prepare for emergencies, especially if you are on an elaborate trip and you do not have a big financial backlog sitting in your bank account, try to get an advance understanding with your bank. If it is already agreed that the bank will lend you up to a specified amount if you need it, you will then be able to activate the deal with a wire or phone call and have the money in your hands within a day or two wherever in the world you may be.

An arrangement like this may cost you nothing if you don't need to use it and get you minimum interest costs if you do. Typical use: you suddenly discover you'd be happier and richer buying a car right now on your trip rather than next month or next year, as you had previously planned. It could happen on a long vacation when the old car breaks down and it does not seem worthwhile to pay for extensive repairs.

Yes, indeed, the friendly banker will bank a trip, and your fun can thus be his business.

To cover smaller or short-time fiscal shortages (meaning: you're broke and there's no more in your bank account either) it is worthwhile to have a guaranteed-overdraft arrangement with your bank even if you do not care to have one while you're home.

This is the kind of plan under which your checks up to a certain total will be honored even if your money has run out. It's an automatic loan with the advantage of involving no extra fees, minimums, or special arrangements — but it does carry a tough 18% interest rate.

If you must let it run on very long, better get a regular loan at half the interest rate and use that money to pay it off. But a charge of a nickel a day per hundred dollars, used cautiously, certainly beats having your checks bouncing all over your hometown. A mere slip in arithmetic can easily cause this to happen when you're off vacationing.

How to use personal checks

Don't overlook the value of an ordinary personal check wherever you travel. Although you can't usually cash one easily where you are not known, it is easy to use one in most stores (abroad too) if you make a major purchase and suggest that the merchandise be sent to your home after your check has cleared.

Chances are that the check will clear and your purchase arrive before you return from your vacation.

In our domestic travels we've often found that you need a driver's license, a local guarantor, and an honest face to cash even a small check for the day's groceries. But when we travel abroad some amazing things happen.

An emergency medical event in France — a burst appendix, no less — wiped out quite a few hundred dollars of our travel funds. We still had money in the bank back home but the big question was how to get it in a hurry.

A tip from a visiting US sailor sent us to the bartender in the gracious old Hotel Ruhl in Nice, where he thought we might be able to cash a check. It was not only possible but a positive pleasure, so the bartender gave us to understand, while casually accepting a personal check for the substantial sum of $850.

Such a large check from a stranger . . .

"How can you afford to take the risk?" we asked.

"What risk?"

"Well, it could be a bad check."

"That would be your problem, not mine," he replied. "It would be you who had made the bad check, not me."

CHAPTER VI

The Well-Nourished Traveler

Good eating makes for good vacationing, but it's no fun to arrive home and find that the only thing thinner than when you set out is your pocketbook.

No one — not even a voracious teenager — should pack away three heavy meals a day, with snacks between, while undergoing no more exertion than riding in a vehicle. Most travelers fare well on a single big meal a day, preferably eaten at midday for the sake of budget as well as health. Most restaurants serve much the same meals at noon as in the evening but charge little more than half as much for them.

To avoid wasting money and food in a restaurant that does not offer children's portions, ask to have one full-course meal divided between two children.

A very young traveler may be happier if you bring along his familiar plastic dish from home. And having it will permit you to serve him small amounts of suitable foods from any of the adult orders. Or bring along his own food and ask to have it warmed.

When we traveled with our four youngsters in Denmark we quickly learned to follow the custom of our Danish cousins who often ordered fewer meals than there were people in the group. The waitress was asked to serve the food family style so that each person could take the amount that fitted his appetite.

Chinese restaurants have long supplied diners, on request, with cartons to carry away uneaten tidbits; other restaurants gladly supply "doggy" bags. Your family can follow suit in any restaurant by carrying along a plastic bag or two. It's easy to carry away uneaten food you've paid for and eat it as snacks later on.

Another way to cut food costs while traveling is *faire le pique-nique,* French style. Stock up with delicacies of the area at a delicatessen and then locate a scenic spot in the countryside. Bring along a folding table, a pretty cloth, and attractive dishes. A picnic tastes better when it's eaten elegantly instead of from cans and bottles stashed on the car's tailgate.

Buying food supplies for travel lunches and snacks is an adventure in itself. A farmer's stand will have fresh fruits and vegetables. In towns, local folk can tell you where to find the best bakery and what the local specialties are.

Memories of good meals or special foods are a part of a successful vacation, too. We remember eating *kolaches* hot from a Czech bakery in Cedar Rapids, Iowa; strawberries the size of plums bought from field-pickers near Salinas, California; cone-shaped sacks of hot, crisp deep-fried miniature fish sold to us by a street vendor in Malaga, Spain; pecan pie in Valdosta, Georgia; anise-flavored bread out of a brick oven in rural Greece.

When you shop for food, seek out small shops or stands even though their prices are a little higher than chain supermarkets. Be careful not to overbuy, because many leftovers cannot be kept safely while in transit.

Avoid buying desserts with restaurant meals unless they are included in the meal price. Buy them, instead, at a bakery or drive-in. You'll save both dollars and pounds.

There are alternatives to conventional eating ways while you're traveling by train or bus, too. Pack a lunch and eat it at your seat instead of bucking the crowd.

Some of the new trains on Amtrak, our national passenger railroad system, now sell sandwiches and drinks but at rather hefty prices.

You eat better on a bus trip if you pick up some local
goodies instead of eating at the bus stop, but. . . .

If you're vacationing by bus there may be an opportunity to buy fruit, rolls and sandwich meat since buses
make frequent 15-minute stops in towns. Then you
could get a little exercise and eat a comparatively
leisurely lunch while you stroll, instead of dashing
into the closest greasy spoon with all the other bus
passengers who want to be served at the same time.

Picnic lunches may even replace airline meal service in the future. Sometime soon you may be able to
fly New York to Europe by "sky train" for $75 a person,
no reservations required, no meals supplied.

To start any trip economically, take along nutritious
snacks from home: tiny cubes of cheese, finger-sized
chunks of melon, small cans of green beans (to be
eaten with the fingers), celery and carrot sticks, crackers, dried dates or prunes cut in half and stuffed with a
dab of peanut butter.

If yours is a vacation by car, make your own break-
fasts to eat before starting or by the roadside as soon
as you find an attractive spot. Buy fruit, rolls, and juice

the night before. Carry powdered milk (individual quart-sized packs are handiest) to be mixed when you're ready to use it.

Pack along a good thermos (the unbreakable metal-lined ones hold liquids boiling hot for 12 or more hours). Have it filled with hot water at a restaurant or motel the night before.

Individual cup-sized packets of cocoa mix, coffee, or tea are handy, avoid spillage and waste.

Reduce calorie intake by combining breakfast and lunch. Then make an early stop for a light dinner. It's well to end the day's driving by mid-afternoon anyway, especially if you have small children and no advance reservation for the night.

There is, unfortunately, no sure-fire way to select a restaurant: and an "award" sign in the window or a flashy chrome front means nothing. A rave mention in a restaurant guidebook can be nullified by an ownership change or the departure of a chef.

Eat where the truckers eat? That ancient advice is unreliable too. Truckers are more interested in the quantity of the food, the quality of the waitresses, and the availability of fat parking spaces than in the things that concern traveling families.

Some pointers that *may* help you spot a good place to eat:

• Ask the local people. (What's the best place in town? What does a meal cost?) We've had this system work equally well in Germany, New Zealand, Indiana, Wyoming.

• A menu posted outside helps you avoid a place where the kinds of meals and prices are completely unsuited to your wants.

• Is the restaurant neat outside, windows clean, paint fresh, landscaping attractive? You can't eat the decor, but it shows that someone cares.

• Let one person step inside before the whole family is committed. He can note whether his nose can quickly spot rancid grease odor, heavy frying, cigarette smoke, and general shabbiness and mustiness.

• Ask for a quick advance inspection of the menu if there's no daily menu posted outside. Beware the too-long menu. Few restaurants can do a good job of serving 30 different time-consuming dishes.

• If it's mealtime, are there other people eating? An almost empty restaurant hints of poor local reputation and such slow business that you may get food that's been reheated or kept too long.

• Ask to use the restroom. If it's clean and properly supplied with soap and towels this is a hint that management concerns itself with sanitation.

Caution is called for at mealtime, but there's a place for a little venturesomeness too. We'd not like to lose from our family vacation memories the recollection of one "mystery" meal during a campout in Norway. On a gamble we'd purchased a good-sized package

When is "bif" not beef? When it's a whale steak.

of meat, the only meat available in a small country-store freezer. Unable to translate the label we'd taken the precaution to note that the storekeeper smiled and nodded "yes" when we pointed to the children and to our mouths. Besides, *hvalbif* on the label sounded like beef to us — until we got hold of a Norwegian-English dictionary some days later.

Anyway, the meat was tender and delicious, with just a bit of a fishy taste. We'd just eaten — possibly invented — our first whale Stroganoff.

CHAPTER VII

Leg-Power Vacationing

Whether you stroll, hike, climb or bicycle, your legs are the key to a free vacation — free in spirit, comparatively free of cost and excellent for your health.

Walk ambitiously and your legs can take you as far as those of the Boy Scout who took two years to walk from South America to the US. Or to similar adventures as those recounted by Colin Fletcher, author of *The Complete Walker*, whose legs took him through Death Valley and on a hiker's-first — a walk through the Grand Canyon.

To publicize the joys of walking, 300 members of the Sierra Club, young and old, recently took a one-night trek through Manhattan to demonstrate that walking can be fun in a city. They started at 11 p.m., ended the walk at 6:30 a.m. with a ride on the Staten Island ferry.

It's well to get your legs into condition beforehand. Start by exploring the streets in your home town. For those who take a bus to work, a walk to the second or third bus stop before getting on is a good conditioner. Driving? Park a mile from the job.

If you find that walking bores you at first, learn to walk with a purpose. One walker we know packs a mini-camera, snaps weirdly garbed tourists from behind, says the pictures will be a book some day. An ecology-oriented family carries trash bags and sticks with nails on the tips to snag soft-drink-can tabs and candy wrappers.

Each family member can do his own walking thing. Twenty fairly brisk minutes of walking equals a mile. Soon you'll be in shape for some real vacation walking.

Plan ahead, so that your walks are meaningful. Here are suggestions on where to walk (the appendix will tell you how to get any information needed):

• Walk the banks of rivers and lakes near you. Explore old and abandoned roads and paths.

• Walk the wilderness. Walk through or around a swamp. Seek out and walk along animal runs.

• Walk the paths of history. There'll be 16 national

trails eventually. Already your family can walk the cattle routes of the West, hike in the steps of the Mormons from Illinois to Utah, follow the footsteps of Lewis and Clark, walk Civil War or Revolutionary War battlefields.

• Climb to the top of a volcano. Lassen Peak in northern California (last eruption in 1917, now becoming active again) has a walking path to the crater. Or walk up 3-year-old Mauna Ula, in Hawaii Volcanoes National Park.

• Walk the desert (but cautiously). Explore old ghost towns.

• Explore our national and state parks. Walk a segment, or all, of the 2,000-mile Appalachian Trail from Maine to Georgia. This four-foot wide trail is the longest marked walking path in the world. In the West, there's the mountainous Pacific Crest Trail, 2,000 miles long and two feet wide, from Canada to Mexico. You can sample short segments of it. Walk the 80 miles of Cape Hatteras National Seashore, North Carolina. Or the marked path along Cape Cod National Seashore. Carry along a good paperback book on beachcombing. Not a continuous walk, but great in segments: the beach of the Pacific Coast from Mexico to Canada.

• Any old canals in your area? Look for towpaths. They're level, peaceful, often overgrown and ready for rediscovery by walkers. Most famous—the Chesapeake and Ohio Canal walk.

• Walk from one town to the next on an old railroad bed. There are many no longer in use. Spark the walk by searching for old bottles or bits of pale blue glass

Vacations are more fun when they take you to
environments that are new to you.

from insulators on electric wires. An undamaged bot-
tle, colored by years in the sun, or an insulator, can be
worth quite a few dollars.
• Walk into the country on skis or snowshoes. No
exceptional skill is called for but you'll need some
stamina to make a mile or more an hour. This is a great
way for families to observe nature, explore and identify
animal tracks and habits.

Best footgear for walking is well-broken-in, ankle-high, broad-toed boots with big eyelets for easy lacing. Many experienced hikers prefer the kind with Vibram soles and heels. Tennis shoes and moccasins soak through, are too flimsy for foot safety. The high heels of cowboy boots can lead to a twisted ankle.

Wear two pairs of socks at a time — perhaps an outer pair of wool, an inner pair of cotton or silk. Carry spares, change frequently to avoid blisters.

In warm weather wear a knit cotton shirt. Carry along a wool shirt and a lightweight sweater for adjustment to the weather. Many walkers like the fishnet undershirt, cool in summer, warm in winter.

For cold weather walking, a nylon jacket, filled with goose down or dacron. Take a nylon rainjacket with hood. One type folds into its own pocket, another zips into a belt. Or get a poncho. It will cover you and your gear, has grommets for converting it into a shelter-tarp.

Other essentials include: compass (learn how to use it before you go), pocket knife, dark glasses, flashlight, sunscreen lip balm in stick form, strip tape bandages, waterproof matches in a metal box, a few sheets of toilet paper, a small water canteen, a bandanna or hat, high-calorie snacks, a map.

Not essential, but enjoyable, especially for children, is a pedometer.

Should you carry a shelter? Experts say yes, even if the walk is intended to be only a one-day family outing. Change of weather, accident, or getting lost needn't be a crisis then. A good nylon tent with water-proof outer roof need add no more than two or three pounds to a load.

A share of the load for the dog

Each hiker, even the family dog, can be individually fitted with a pack proper for his shape, height, weight. Don't overload. Even a ten-pound pack can become a burden to a beginner by the end of a long walk.

Go prepared for weather change — plenty of warm clothing, emergency shelter, matches, stove, rations. Let someone know where you're headed and when you expect to return. (This goes for good weather walking, too, of course.)

Bicycles are kid stuff no more and bicycle vacation-ing on a national scale is getting a boost through state and local expenditures for special bicycle roads or paths. Europe — especially flat countries like Holland, Belgium and Denmark, with paved bike roads — has long been paradise for bicycling families.

The least expensive way to get started on bicycling is with rented bikes. Used ones often can be had at $20 or less. For good buys check the classifieds, bulletin boards in supermarkets and around colleges, or attend the annual police auction, when unclaimed bicycles go for low prices.

There are many magnificent ten-speed $200-or-more bicycles for touring, but you don't need one of these, especially at first. Grandparents, and even great grandparents, can go. (There's a three-wheeled senior-citizen special you can get through mail-order houses).

Accessories? A bell is longer lasting, more distinctive sounding than a horn. A basket or saddlebag carrier will handle take-alongs. A bolt-on backseat for a toddler costs a few dollars. An old-fashioned leg-strap light is a good choice: a thief can't get it, because you don't leave it with the bike.

Register or license your bicycle. Keep the registration number in a safe place.

As a bicycling or walking family you'll be one-up on mere automobile vacationers. State and national parks are beginning to outlaw cars. Access to interior and scenic areas soon will be limited to non-polluting vehicles only.

To get to such places if cycling all the way will take too long, you can equip your car with bike racks, leave it at a designated parking area in a vacation spot, go the rest of the way by bicycle. Consider buying a fold-up or take-apart bike which rides neatly in car trunk or on top. Trains and buses will tote your bikes as luggage, but be sure they're securely tagged.

CHAPTER VIII

On
the
Water

For a vacation on the water you have a wide choice of ways to go, ranging from canoe through outboard cruiser, power boat, yacht, houseboat, luxury cruise liner.

Houseboats are currently among the most popular vehicles because they offer the comfort of a home and yet piloting one is a low-pressure art that you can quickly learn if you can drive a car — or even if you can't. The result is that all over the US, rivers, lakes and coastal waterways have become house-boating territory for vacationing families.

Since a houseboat costs from $20,000 to $50,000, rental is the obvious approach. Even if you can buy, and would like to eventually, several test vacations are in order first. You can usually arrange to have rent payments applied to purchase cost if you do decide to buy.

Rents range from $200 to $500 a week, making quite substantial the 20 to 30% you save by going out of season: between Labor Day and April 1. Life on the water can be especially pleasant in fall and spring

Recommended for landlubbers seeking adventures on the water: houseboats, because they are more house than boat.

when houseboaters are relatively scarce. And since houseboats sleep up to ten people, you can reduce rental cost further by sharing with one or two families.

Before you leave the dock, you'll be given a shake-down cruise, operating instructions, detailed water-chart information, and tips on houseboat living. This will be your chance to find out both just what is included and how it works. You'll want to make sure there is safety equipment including life vests for all on board, a functioning water system (safe for drinking as well as bathing), linens, dishes, cooking equipment. Twin engines and auxiliary fuel and water tanks are good safety features.

Not every houseboat is fully self-sufficient. Find out whether yours is equipped so you can tie up comfortably or anchor nearly anywhere or whether you'll have to locate a marina each night for electric and sewer connections.

Camping, boating and travel magazines and newspaper classifieds under boat rentals will help you find the right water area and the right houseboat. Or you can go directly to a convenient marina for information.

One example of what you might look for: Bullfrog Resort and Marina, at Hanksville, Utah, offers a fully equipped 43-foot houseboat that sleeps nine. Off-season you save 20% on the $400-a-week rental. You can tour hundreds of watery miles near the red rock cliffs on Lake Powell, formed when the Glen

Canyon Dam was constructed on the Colorado River.

Some of the best houseboating areas: California, Florida, Minnesota, almost everywhere along the Great Lakes and major rivers.

For a less expensive but more rugged water vacation, try a canoe trip. You can buy or rent lightweight canoes. Made of aluminum or fiberglass, they ride to point of launching on a car top, are easy to portage, or carry across land, and highly resistant to damage.

Canoeing calls for lightweight gear for all kinds of weather. It also calls for respect for the outdoors (because you may be traveling in wilderness areas rarely seen by man), quite a bit of stamina and some swimming ability. For extra safety, this last should be supplemented by a life vest.

Any gentle river, stream or lake is good for canoeing. One trip to consider: through the National Boundary Water Canoe Area, 1,062,000 acres with more than a thousand miles of canoe "trail." It's located in the border country between Minnesota and Canada. Or contemplate paddling through the Allagash Wilderness waterway in Maine, with thousands of acres of forest around you to explore. Figure that costs will run $10 a day and up per person, including equipment, instruction and sometimes food.

The appendix tells you where to write for information on canoe and other water trips, such as float trips, wild and tame. These vary from riding the rough Colorado to floating gentle Snake River at Jackson Hole, Wyoming, where young children can take part safely.

Another way to vacation by water is a combined auto-boat trip. Drive to a body of water with a ferry system. Here's one that makes a great West Coast family vacation. Camp along the Pacific all the way through California, Oregon, and Washington (there are state parks along all the beaches for a thousand miles).

A stay in Alaska should include a seaborne junket which will give you close-ups of icebergs.

Then take a ferry from Port Angeles, Washington, to Victoria, B.C., on Vancouver Island. Camp again to the end of the road at Kelsey Bay where you can board the *Queen of Prince Rupert* and sail to Alaska.

Or drive to Seattle, Washington, as an alternative, and go the rest of the way to Skagway, Alaska, by ship.

Beyond Alaska there's the Blue Star Cruise which sidles up to Le Conte Glacier and thousands of icebergs — charges $17.50 for adults, half price for children.

On the East Coast you can drive up to Maine and take a car ferry to Nova Scotia, giving you a scenic and

restful break in driving. Cruise boats go in and out of many harbors, from Canada to Florida and the Bahamas. Generally, the larger the ship the more service and luxury you get. Family budget permitting, there's no better place to relax than on board ship — no smog, no traffic and a chance for a family to be together and independent at the same time. Children can't get lost on a ship and often there's special food and entertainment for them with no need for parental supervision.

Want to cruise on your own yacht? Although J. P. Morgan once said that if you have to ask the cost of owning a yacht you can't afford one, there are people who defray the cost of such ownership by chartering out their yachts to people like you and us. If you've had experience with a boat and can provide evidence that you're responsible along with a substantial deposit in case you're not, you can rent a yacht. You'll probably want to take along another family to help as crew as well as share costs.

There are sailing schools (see *Appendix*) with family rates that come to about $100 a person. Classified ads in boat-area newspapers regularly offer reduced cruise rates to those who can serve as crew.

Cheapest water travel of all is the ferryboat ride. Sometimes you can get snacks or even a good meal on board. One outdoorsy family tells us they use the lavish hot water supply in ferryboat washrooms for a sponge bath or even a hair wash if they've been camping where such comforts weren't easily come by.

Should you ever venture far enough to vacation in the lake country north of Helsinki, Finland, you can get the greatest ferry bargain of all — a free ride for you and your car, too. Where one segment of the highway disappears into a lake, all travelers are ferried, without charge, across to where the road begins again. Who could ask for anything more?

Another great bargain is New York's Staten Island Ferry. Sail back and forth forever if you wish. Kids love it. Or, if you find yourself in Turkey, take the Istanbul ferry that, for the equivalent of a few cents, takes you from one continent to another.

CHAPTER IX

Down on the Farm

Working ranches and farms by the hundreds are now organized to salt your vacation weeks with new experiences. You can learn to mend fences, ride trails, explore deep canyons, prepare real cowboy food, help with the harvest, feed animals, get produce ready for market, assist with its sale at a roadside stand, and maybe even brand cattle and bust broncos.

(Again, check the appendix for information in print on locating a farm or ranch that appeals to you.)

It's quite possible to find a suitable farm or ranch by driving to an area that attracts you, and make inquiries locally about the possibility of bringing your recreational vehicle, or pitching a tent, and staying for a period at a local ranch.

Just drop in and chat for awhile with a farmer. If he's not open to your offer, he's quite likely to know someone who will be.

If you bring your own camper or station wagon or car-plus-tent, you'll find this an economical way to experience great outdoor ranch living. For as little as a dollar a night per adult, half that much for each child, you'll be given a place to set up your own quarters. The fee usually includes water, electricity, sanitary facilities.

If you fly in, or come by train or bus, the ranch may put you up in a bunkhouse, log cabin, or dormitory. Costs vary a good deal, but you'll still pay only a fraction of what you would at a luxury hotel where you might have just half the fun and far less to remember later on.

The choice among ranches is a wide one. You might choose historic Diamond Guest Ranch in Wyoming, 75,000 acres in the foothills of the Snowy Range of the Rockies. At a total fee of $5 a night for 6 (50 cents for each additional person) you can set up your own camping rig, swim, ride the trails, fish, hunt, go to the Saturday night barn dance, or just loll in the lounge and get acquainted with other families.

Not all ranches are in the West. The 2,100-acre

Combine camping with a stay at a ranch
and the diversions offered you run a wide gamut.

Triangle S Ranch in Southern Kentucky offers hay-rides, horseshoes, square dancing, fishing, boating, riding, hiking.

Want to see Alaska? Newly opened McKinley-Healy Ranch at Mile 248.5, Anchorage-Fairbanks Highway, will give your family a view of the fragile Arctic tundra, let you visit Alaska's largest coal mine near by, and enjoy peace and quiet. Bring your own camping outfit and all this will cost you $4.50 a night for two, 25 cents extra for each additional person.

If you're not do-it-yourself rugged-living types, you can spend more money and let someone else do the chores. For example, a family can play pioneer for a week with the wagon outfit that works the Old Butterfield Trail. Six to 22 of their Conestoga wagons cross 20 miles of prairie daily in summer. At night, bunks and tents are set up for sleeping, the wagons pull into a circle for campfires and a traditional meal. During the day there are stagecoach rides, fossil hunting, sightseeing: old forts, a sod house, etc.

For this adventure the cost is nearly $200 per adult, about half that for each child. (Again, see the appendix.)

Robber's Roost Ranch is 205,000 acres of old outlaw hideout near Green River, Utah. Butch Cassidy's gang hid there, and famous western author Zane Grey wrote about it. You can fly in (there's a 2,500 foot airstrip next to the ranch house) or you can drive.

The Roost offers 4-wheel-drive car trips, hikes to red rock buttes, explorations of pre-Columbian canyon painting, rides on an old Spanish trail of the 1500s. Ranch hosts are experts on geology, pictographs, petroglyphs (rock carvings). Adults pay $32.50 a day, children half price, but if you fit in with ranch work and help a little you can shave $7.50 a day from the cost.

For some, a farm may be more appealing than a ranch.

Hundreds of farms in all fifty states, plus Canada, welcome paying guests — sometimes in winter as well as summer.

Prices reflect what you get, ranging from as little as $55 a week per adult (half that for children), all meals included, to a high of $200 a week.

Many farm families are genuinely less interested in profit than in excitement and a change from the farm routine that ties them down in the summer. Their children want to meet your children; ages of the children on the farm are often noted in listings. Teenagers who want to cut vacation costs can sometimes arrange to do so by helping with farm chores.

Some things you might do as farm guests: milk a cow, help plant and harvest an organic garden, see kittens and calves born, observe artificial insemination, pan for gold, hunt fossils, dig for old bottles, enjoy piano, organ, and instrumental music, care for a horse matched to your riding ability, dig in Indian ruins, help tend a vegetable stand, learn about Mennonite families in Amish country, see the highest tide in the world — 40 feet — at a Nova Scotia farm on Cobequid Bay, help make ice cream, learn to bake bread, attend a livestock auction.

Vacation farm choices should be made in winter or early spring by an exchange of letters with owners, setting a date, making a deposit, indicating special desires or needs. Since most farms take only a few families each year, guests and hosts often become personal friends, and a short vacation may bring you lifelong friendships.

Families that have enjoyed farm vacations offer these pointers:
• Take plenty of old clothes and extra shoes for mud and wet fields.

• Unless promised, don't count on a private bath or toilet. Facilities may be down the hall, on another floor, or even outdoors.
• Be prepared to fit in with the farm routine instead of expecting the farm to adjust to your habits.
• Go easy on consumption of water. The well may be running low, especially toward the end of a dry season.
• Help out now and then, whether required to or not. Gathering eggs, picking fruit, digging vegetables makes eating them more fun.
• Remember that farm families must go to bed early and get up early. Try to go along.

Finally, you'll enjoy your stay more if you try to behave like a thoughtful guest rather than a demanding customer.

On a farm vacation a city-dweller gets the opportunity to test her mettle with non-city-dwellers.

CHAPTER X

Camping Here and Abroad

Camping is the way to a bargain-priced family vacation — so we're often told. Yet many families have gone camping only to reckon later that they'd have been money ahead if they'd loafed at a resort hotel instead.

Camping may be the way to a carefree vacation — no prearrangements, no reservations. But the "No Vacancy" sign is no longer a rarity in national and state parks and forest campgrounds. Some families even find themselves booking space for their tent months ahead.

This seems to be a contradiction. How come?

The cost paradox springs from the fact that even deluxe camping equipment represents a modest investment — if amortized over many weeks of use. But if you use that fine nylon tent and those down-filled sleeping bags only once or twice before abandoning the whole idea, you'll have spent hundreds of dollars for a few nights in the woods.

And that carefree goeth-where-thou-listeth aspect depends upon time and place. Camping can still be spur-of-the-moment, but not if you choose a popular beach park at Easter.

Camping equipment is no extravagance if you make real use of it. Consider that, by American Automobile Association reckoning, an ordinary trip for two will run you $33 a day, about equally divided between meals and motel. When you camp, however, over-night lodging in a state or national park, usually with hot shower, costs only $1 to $3 even for a large family. To the extent that you cook your own meals, food need cost no more than it does at home, assuming shopping is carefully done and meals are simple.

So you can own first-rate camping equipment and still be money ahead, if you use the equipment on many vacations. If you're not sure, start with a trial campout — overnight or a weekend — with equipment borrowed from friends or rented.

This holds true for any new camping equipment
— home-made or store-bought. Consider the experience of a family who camped next to us at Furnace
Creek in Death Valley.

They'd created a tepee some fifteen feet tall, all
with their own hands. It was handsewn, hand-deco-
rated with Indian symbols, a painting among tents,
a work of art — until the wind began to come up in
the evening.

Desert gusts, sweeping in about sunset, tore their
tent to the ground as soon as they'd erected it. All

These tenderfeet, see, deciding to go in for camping,
didn't buy a tent. They handmade a replica of a
tepee. And then the wind came up.

hands pitched in to assemble poles and spread canvas again and again, but in the end there was nothing for our neighbors to do but sleep on air mattresses on the cold sand under the most inadequate protection of their fallen creation.

You may be able to rent with rental fee going toward purchase, if you then decide to plunge.

The truth is, camping's not for everybody. Before you acquire all that delightful equipment and start your family on the camping route, ask yourself and the rest of the family the questions that follow.

---

1) Why do we want to go camping?

2) How much can we afford to spend?

3) Will this be the first of many camping trips, or a one-time experiment?

4) Where do you want to camp? Close to home? Across the country? Abroad?

5) Do we expect home comforts or can we enjoy — as well as endure — chilly weather, campfire cooking, sleeping on the ground?

6) What kind of camping grounds do we like? In parks? On private grounds? In the wilderness?

7) How much equipment do we now own? How much do we need to buy?

8) Do we want to go tenting with a car? Or hike? Or bike?

9) Are all members of the family the right ages to enjoy camping?

10) How does camping compare for us with other possible vacations?

Essentially there are two kinds of camping by car. One is the destination camp where you'll spend a vacation period. The other is the overnight stop on the way to where you're planning to spend the rest of your vacation.

It isn't going to matter too much whether an overnight camp has swimming, hiking, and a scenic outlook. You'll use it primarily as an economical motel under canvas. You'll want it close to the highway, clean and with facilities for bathing.

Traditional private campgrounds and the motel-campgrounds that are springing up everywhere fill these needs. You can even reserve space ahead of time, often with a toll-free call from one stop to the next.

In most scenic and park areas there are numerous campsites just off the road that are pleasant and easy for one or several nights. But real camping begins with choosing a spot where you want to spend a good part of your vacation. It can be quite civilized or charmingly primitive.

On the deluxe side, it could be a space in a national park with stone fireplace, table and benches, modern washrooms with hot water, planned hikes guided by a ranger, nightly nature talks, numerous recreational

When you're camping, one of the biggest problems
is the drinking water. *Is* it drinking water?

facilities and a store where you can buy souvenirs
and groceries.

Or it may be in a national forest that offers isola-
tion, dramatic scenery, wild animals, and no facilities
other than a safe stream from which to drink.

But don't take anything for granted in this respect.
Always take a few minutes to check out your source
of drinking water even if you have every reason to
believe it's safe. A Texas family, camped in a high
meadow camp of Lassen National Park, were reas-
sured by an official sign informing them that the clear
mountain stream was for drinking and general camp
use, but not for laundry. They drank the water.

In the evening cool they strolled uphill and at the highest campsite of all discovered a young woman casually rinsing out her baby's diapers in the stream that flowed down to other campsites.

A park ranger took care of that woman's crime, and in no uncertain terms, but our friends have been inclined to do their own personal checkups — in advance — on water supplies ever since.

Reliable guidebooks to camping sites have begun to abound in recent years, as the appendix shows.

The growing popularity of camping has led to over-crowding. National and state parks may have a "Camp Full" or "No Vacancy" sign out by mid-afternoon during the summer and some holiday weekends. Some states have a reservation system, and you have to reserve your campsite at a popular beach park on January 1, when reservations open for the coming year. In at least one state, campers from out-of-state are on a quota basis.

Because of congestion and wear-and-tear on facilities, some national parks have begun to ban automobile traffic. Campers must leave their vehicles outside the park and hike in to pitch their tents. The situation is growing worse as more and more families turn to camp-ing as a means of combatting the high cost of other vacations.

The approach to a very popular public camping area
on a popular camping holiday, e.g., Easter.

The savvy camper will soon discover ways to over-come this problem. The simplest way is to go off-season. Another is to look for smaller, less-known sites not far from the famous — and crowded — ones.

We tried for a beach camp one Easter. No chance. A ranger suggested we go inland a few miles. There we found not one but several small state parks with excellent campgrounds where there was more than enough room.

Another way to lick the "full-up" problem is to equip yourself well enough so that you can comfortably use the camps with so few facil-ities and amenities that they are necessarily passed up by most families.

You will find many such simple forest campgrounds in the heavily wooded areas that surround state and national parks.

Acquiring a campsite of your own is another solu-tion to the crowded-world problem. Consider buying a little piece of land now — before the price goes even higher — in a place where you might build a cabin someday. You can begin to clear brush and otherwise improve your property during camping vacations. As we did not long ago, you might con-struct a permanent wooden deck on which to erect your tent, with room to place tables and chairs. To simplify construction we hauled in pre-assembled decking made of redwood two-by-fours assembled into three-foot and four-foot squares.

As you might expect, the farther you go from heavily populated areas the more space you'll find available. In large parts of the desert, campsites are there to be used, but risks go with them. Don't just drive off the paved road without investigating the validity of the terrain. Don't take a quaint desert road without carrying adequate supplies. If you're going camping in an isolated area let someone know: a ranger, a nearby gas-station or store owner.

In fenced country, get permission from a rancher or farmer to use his land for the night. Assurance that you'll leave no litter — and perhaps that you'll build no fires — may help clinch the deal.

In an emergency — let's say you've driven too far and no campground is in sight — ask the highway patrol people for advice. They don't want you on the road if you're exhausted any more than you want to be there.

We have been escorted by police to campsites we'd never have found ourselves. In Montana they sent us to an Old Settler's Park. We had to agree to let the caretaker lock the gates behind us for the night — "to be sure no vandals get in," he said. We spent the night in complete privacy. The caretaker opened the gate for us before 6 in the morning.

Sites marked "picnics only" often can be used for an overnight stop — with permission.

A fairly new way of camping is non-tenting camping, i.e., using a Recreational Vehicle — RV — not only

The local officials willingly granted permission to camp in a park, and locked up the park as part of the normal procedures for preventing vandalism.

to get there but to provide shelter, beds, cooking and bathroom facilities when you get there. The boom in RVs is creating a whole new industry. Its devotees are not campers in the ordinary sense; in fact, they've been known to refer to tenters as the "Me Tarzan" crowd.

If you join them — by using a truck with camp-accessory top, a trailer, or some version of the mini-home on wheels — you'll be limited in areas allowing you to drive there. Although you may find you're not welcome in some parks, you'll discover, however, that a great many others are set up especially for you. Private campgrounds and chain motel-campgrounds cater to the RV family.

Camping vehicles are particularly good for real
wilderness trips — Alaska, Mexico, northern
Canada. You're in rough country, but you
aren't roughing it.

The basic problem with an RV, of course, is the size
of your investment: thousands of dollars instead of
hundreds tied up in camping equipment. This may
be hard to justify unless you will use the vehicle for
many weeks of the year or can rent it out when you're
not using it. Depreciation on recreational vehicles is
generally heavy. Don't figure on using yours for a
year or two and recovering your investment. More
likely you'll take a beating.

Rent before you buy

Expensive though RV rentals tend to be, you might
still be better off renting than buying, especially
before you're sure how the whole thing will work out.

One way around the high cost is to acquire an RV
with dual-use possibilities. A pick-up with removable
camper body is no extravagance if you need a truck
anyway. A very small RV, such as a Volkswagen Campmobile, may serve most of the year as a regular family
car.

There are many publications to advise you where
to go in RVs and what RVs to go there in. The appendix will guide you to them.

Can you visualize touring the back roads of Norway in an RV? Or cooking outdoors at the foot of an Alp? Or tenting among a thousand other travelers from all over the world in a great park in Paris or London?

Why not?

A tour of Europe can be an unforgettable adventure for a family. Camping adds to the richness of the experience while making an extended tour economically feasible for just about any family that can put together the time. A camping tour of Europe need cost no more than staying home and dreaming about it.

We made our first trip of this kind a dozen years ago. It still comes to life at gatherings of the clan. Along with treasured private memories — the first, unexpected, glimpse of the "Winged Victory" in the Louvre, bicycling around Amsterdam at rush hour — we find many shared ones.

The watered tire, the man with balloons

"The look on that man's face in Germany when we rolled that flat tire in and all that water poured out." (None of us had enough German to explain that this, our second flat of the day, had caught us without a spare. And that one of our teenage daughters, helping her father roll the wheel toward the distantly seen village, had let it get away and plunge into the Danube).

"What about that other time we had to change a tire, in Spain, and we drew such a crowd that a man came and sold balloons?"

"I liked that crowd better than the one we drew

in Morocco. Do you think those shepherds really would have hurt us?" (We decamped so hurriedly, just in case, that one of our party was still brushing her teeth as our camper rocked down the road.)

Camping summers from Portugal to Finland are not new — for Europeans. For German, Scandinavian, and British families especially, camping is the normal way to take a vacation trip. That's one of the reasons Americans on ordinary, or hotel-stop, tours meet mostly fellow Americans.

Fond memories are the dividends of a family vacation.
Example: the astonishment of a German service-
station operator on delivery of a flat tire full of
water. To find out how the tire got that way, read the text.

Why is a European tour suddenly something that just about any family can manage, given sufficient determination and joint effort? The answer is three-fold.

One is the growth of charter and other bargain flights that slash the cost of getting to Europe and back — in many cases to less than half what it used to be.

A second is the great increase in the number of comfortable and secure camping sites in Europe. Hotel-going with children is painful at best, but camping can be mutual fun for all members of the family. On the feasibility side, please note that camping not only knocks a hotel bill of ten or twenty dollars down to a camp fee of a dollar or so; it also permits cooking at a fraction of the price of restaurant meals.

The third factor that makes all this possible for more is the new availability of equipment rentals. These include specialized camping vehicles, cars with tents, cars or tents alone, and even such small items as stoves, lamps, sleeping bags and stools.

Begin your planning to camp in Europe with the question of wheels.

A bus with a pop-up top

The ideal way to travel and camp in Europe is by a modification of, or variation on, the well-known Volkswagen bus. Along with sink, icebox, cupboards,' and closets, it provides sleeping space for two adults and several children. For more people — or more spaciousness — a fasten-on tent can be had. Another option is a pop-up top for headroom while dressing or cooking.

The other way to go is by ordinary automobile, carrying a tent or two for sleeping. Being real camping, this is in some ways more fun (for camping nuts) than using a camping vehicle; it is also more difficult, especially with small children. Families that have already camped together will know whether they are adapted to this degree of roughing it.

We've tried both ways, and liked them.

If your economic plan allows for the purchase of a new European car in the year of your trip, you have no problem. Buy at factory price and ship your car home afterward and you will still have spent less than the US price. The use abroad will have cost you nothing, except for gas and oil, of course. The saving on some models will even pay for several fares to Europe and back.

An example: Our last trip came at a time when we were happy to dispose of our family car — eight years old, with 90,000 miles on the odometer. We bought a Fiat at the factory price of $2,738. Shipping it back cost $348, including insurance and freight fees. Duty and excise tax added $186, for a total of $3,682 plus $184 sales tax. The difference between that and the US price more than paid for two round-trip charter fares of $270 each.

An economical alternative is to buy a used car — an ordinary sedan, a station wagon, or a fully equipped campmobile — in Europe, either to resell at a small loss or to bring home.

Buying a used car is just as feasible in Europe as at home — and just as risky. It is probably a good idea only for someone who has bought used cars before or has some technical knowledge about cars.

Whether you buy a used car direct or through a dealer your best bet is one previously owned by an American tourist. These are exempt from local taxes, which are often heavy, and fit American specifi-cations: sealed beam headlights, laminated wind-shield, speedometer in miles. Good buys in used camping vehicles are often available, especially toward the end of summer. In parking areas near American Express offices in big cities you'll often find cars with "tourist must sell" signs on them.

Renting a car or camping equipment in Europe is economical only for short periods: for a two-week trip or for a try-out period.

Who wants to dress up?

The best sources of advice on travel problems in general are the standard travel guides. See your near-est bookstore, public library and suggestions in the appendix of this book. You'll have to modify much of the advice in travel books to make it fit you as a camping family. Unlike most travelers, you'll be taking along such things as a tent, sleeping bags and air mattresses. On the other hand, by avoiding the hotel circuit you will avoid most dress-up occasions and you will be easily able to do your own laundry. Camps provide for such things, hotels do not.

Any travel guide will tell you how to get pass-ports. Bear in mind that if no members of the party will be crossing borders independently, you can use a family passport, with a saving of $12 for each person.

What may strike you ahead of time as the most formidable problem — finding camping places — will prove surprisingly easy. Unlike the US, where camps are pretty much limited to wild areas, Europe has them everywhere. And everywhere means resort areas as well as remote and primitive spots, major cities as well as villages. We can testify to the presence of campgrounds in London, Paris, Copenhagen, Helsinki, Athens, Stockholm, Oslo, Berlin, Hamburg, Edinburgh, Budapest, Rome, Prague, Belgrade, Madrid, Lisbon.

The locations of these camps and some 4,000 more are given in guidebooks available in bookstores in all major European cities. These books print information in several languages, including English, with pictorial symbols to give you a rundown on facilities offered. Thus you will know in advance if a camp is level, hilly, sandy, wooded, if it has a view, and whether — like most camps today — it has flush toilets, hot showers, laundry rooms and a grocery

Metropolitan areas in Europe, unlike those in the
US, have campsites nearby, so there's no excuse to
affront a gendarme in Paris by pitching tent in a *place*.

store. You can also ascertain fees, which average out to fifty cents a person.

Many campers rely on free maps and lists from national tourist offices. And they depend upon spotting a directional camping sign (picture of a tent, with an arrow pointing the way to go, usually found along a main street or highway).

Since camps are even more cosmopolitan in their guests than hotels are, you'll find the language problem seldom arises. Someone always speaks English.

Finally, a prime rule about camping: always, *always* expect the unexpected. You'll seldom be disappointed.

Our four children thought it pretty funny that someone had inscribed a Texas underpass under which we drove our camp vehicle with foot-high crude letters: "Ah hates Texas."

But we began to find out what that unknown traveler meant when the Texas skies dumped a cloudburst on us, only to follow it with a two hour red-dust storm that obliterated the landscape.

Things settled down by evening, so we pulled our tiny trailer into a roadside park, ate beside a pleasant campfire we hardly needed, and then rinsed out our camp duds and hung them to dry in a balmy breeze.

We awoke all too early on a frigid morning to find the Texas panhandle covered with snow. Our tear-

drop trailer was being pelted by hail, our car promptly snapped a fan belt when we started its engine and there were loud complaints from the child whose night it had been to sleep in the tent-annex buckled to its side.

Breakfast was a quart of frozen milk and some chilled Hydrox cookies. We gathered our stiffened

garments from the bushes and made our way to the
nearest town, stopping every mile to cool our engine,
soon overheated for lack of the fan belt.

"It was an experience, but did we need it?" com-
mented one of the girls after the icicles on the under-
pinnings of the car had finally thawed sometime after
noon.

CHAPTER XI

Prepackaged Vacations: Tours and All That

Tours come in three packages: the extravagant, the real bargains and the inevitable.

In the last category come those tours for which there is no reasonable alternative. To view a harbor city from the sea you'll seldom find it feasible to charter a boat. So a ready-made tour is the obvious answer.

City tours by sightseeing bus are also hands-down choices in most places. You can see something of a city from ordinary public transportation or your own car (the driver won't see much) but you won't know where to go and you won't always know what you're looking at.

In many places, sightseeing tours are offered exclusively by the city or national tourist office or by a single company — i.e., there's no competition. But in other places there'll be two or more tour companies outshouting each other for your business. Then you must do some comparison shopping, just as when you make a material purchase.

What's the difference between "Grey" and "Gray"?

Look first of all for reliable sponsorship. In one city, for instance, you may have narrowed down your choice to "The Grey Line Tours" and "The Gray Line." (Note the difference in spelling — and resemblance in sound.)

The latter, you discover after a second and third look at the ad or brochure, is connected with a well-known and reliable name in American travel-services. The former has nothing to recommend it but a carefully selected name.

To tell whether an offered tour falls into category 1 (extravagant) or category 2 (bargain) may call for some arithmetic, which is possibly the reason that many tourists fall for the first type. We committed a splendid example of just this in Mexico City recently.

Without stopping to do arithmetic or make a check on the tour company's reputation or sponsorship, we blithely signed up for a 2-day tour of Cuernavaca and Taxco. What the brochure had rendered as a leisurely and charming couple of days turned out to be:

• A rocketing, swaying drive in an old 5-passenger sedan stuffed with six people. (The passengers in the middle, over the drive shaft, saw almost nothing of the countryside; the unlucky fellow riding left rear kept getting cigarette ash in his eye.)

• A breathless single stop in Cuernavaca, limited to a few minutes by the fact that three of our fellow-tourists were on a one-day version of the tour and had to see Taxco as well by 4 PM.

• Mere minutes for our full-course noon meal, paid for in our tour price, if we were to get in on the Taxco part of the tour at all.

• Beds overnight in a tolerable but cheerless motel too far from town to let us walk there.

• Three edible but uninteresting meals.

• A ride back to Mexico City if we waited till the next afternoon. Having seen enough of Taxco we took the public bus instead, at an hour of our own choosing, and thus found how much more comfortable it was.

Their arithmetic was late

That evening we did our arithmetic, two days late. And discovered we'd paid for just about twice what we got.

A savvy traveler's budget would have gone like this: cabs to the bus station from our hotel and back again the next day, about $5; tickets for two on the air-conditioned deluxe public bus, to Cuernavaca, Taxco and return, $8; cabs in the two towns, $3; beds and three meals in the motel, $24.

For this far more comfortable trip and flexible schedule we'd have paid $40 instead of the tour price of $68 for two. By skipping two of the cab rides in favor of Mexico City's new and splendid subway we could have cut the cost another $4 and added an interesting experience.

Despite this disheartening swindle, we know of tour packages that are quite remarkable bargains — the kind that add up to far more than the sum of their parts. These come most notably in airline offerings that bundle together air tickets, car rentals and hotel rooms. To make a financial assessment of one of these packages you must begin by estimating the value of each part.

But it is not enough to determine the cash cost. What you want to know is the actual value to you. If it is located somewhere you don't plan to go, even the finest hotel room has a value of precisely zero. Indeed, the hotel part of many tour packages is what the travel trade calls a "throwaway" — a feature put in to look good or make the pricing legal but not likely to be used.

But don't scorn a package just because some of it may be throwaway for you; what remains can still be a bargain. One friend of ours, planning a half-year in Europe, found the best bargain for her was to buy a round-trip air ticket that included a three-week bus-and-hotel tour of Portugal (which fitted her plans nicely as a beginning for her season abroad). After the three weeks she threw away the return ticket and went on her own, and was money ahead compared to purchasing a one-way full-fare ticket to Europe and transportation and hotels for the initial three weeks.

Best of all, obviously, is the no-throwaway — the package so well designed — from your point of view — that you'll be glad to use every part.

CHAPTER XII

Live like
the Very Rich,
for a While

Living like the very rich for a little while is a pleasure open to anyone who exercises a little ingenuity.

A multimillionaire can't use all his houses and his boats at the same time. Nor can he simultaneously occupy all the rooms in a luxurious resort. He needs you to help support his yacht and his vacation home.

And even a great gourmet restaurant can't survive on the millionaires' custom alone.

So there's "a touch of mink" waiting for you if you know where to look. In a marina on Guadaloupe, a

Caribbean island a short flight from New York, is the 80-foot Diogene II, once owned by King Farouk, once ruler of Egypt. For $126 a day up to 9 people (plus possibly a small child or two) can set sail in sybaritic fashion. The price includes a crew. With two or three families sharing the cost it could come to as little as about $14 a day per person, the price of a mediocre room in an ordinary hotel.

Charter the princess's yacht

Would you like to cruise on a yacht built by Aristotle Onassis for Princess Grace of Monaco? It's for charter, too. (Her Royal Highness, alas, never set foot on the yacht because of a rift that developed between Onassis and the rulers of Monaco.)

Ask your travel agent, or look around any marina in resort waters for interesting yachts available for charter. Many are available when their owners aren't using them.

Or consider a vacation on a tropical island, such as Freeport in the Bahamas, with its elegant condominium resort at Lucaya. While the jet-setters are off jetting you can get at a reasonable rent a penthouse or one of the other condominiums with a view of the blue sea and white sand from your windows. Maid service is included. (See the appendix for further information.)

How about making an authentic castle your home away from home? In Germany and Austria it's a *Schloss*, in Holland a *kasteel*, in France a *chateau*, in Spain a *parador*. In any language it's a bargain: $7 to $15 a day per person, including all three meals.

Sometimes you can meet the noble owner himself, when the count, baron, or duke is in residence, as the duke and his duchess are at Woburn Abbey, located in Bedfordshire, England. This castle has been the home of the dukes of Bedford for three centuries. Kings and queens have slept there. You can see art treasures valued in the millions and 3,000 acres of surrounding park plus zoological gardens, and often the duke himself supervising the premises.

Have dinner with the duke and duchess

For a small sum you can wander the park and tour the house. If you're willing to go all out for one night of high living you can spend $155 a person and be entertained at a formal dinner with the present (13th) duke and duchess as your host and hostess at the table. And you'll be given a noble's suite for the night.

Where chivalry once flourished, you can be a tenant.

(A number of ducal homes in England have been opened to visitors: high inheritance and income taxes.)

Another grand-scale home is the Schloss Mittersill, near Salzburg, Austria. You need an introduction from someone who will vouch for you to be entertained here, where guests have included maharajas, queens, and lesser nabobs. For a $1,000 fee, if this is your thing, you can join an exclusive club with lifetime privileges at the *Schloss*.

Most castles are not this grand in price. Many have turrets, moats, dungeons, hunting grounds, knight's hall, perhaps a ghost or two.

The one true storybook castle in the US located on Highway 1, halfway between Los Angeles and San Francisco, was built for the late newspaper tycoon William Randolph Hearst. It's now a California state park and open for half-day and all-day tours (Christmas and New Year's excepted). There's a magnificent pool, furniture and art objects worth millions, and parts of ancient buildings brought over stone by stone from Europe and reconstructed authentically.

Off-season and bargaining bonuses are available to those willing or able to vacation in spring or fall, just when weather may be at its best in many areas. Service may be better then, too, in the absence of crowds.

One of the fondest of our own family vacation memories is of the week we were offered a half-price deal for an elegant suite with kitchenette at a beachfront hotel in Florida. We had perfect weather, a large beach to ourselves, and prompt and relaxed service from a staff with few other guests to wait upon.

Big city hotels like to boost business in summer, especially on weekends, when "everyone" leaves town. Cut rates, special deals for families, extras such as a champagne breakfast in one's room, fruit and flowers gratis, tickets to special events — these are things to look for. Ask a travel agent about these package bargains, or write directly to a hotel that interests you.

Go out of season if you can.

Bargain on the spot. It often works. An American schoolteacher traveling with wife and brood of four, on sabbatical leave at half-pay, found it quite feasible to stay for a month at a resort near Athens, Greece, for less than it would have cost at a mediocre tourist hotel.

Where the Onassis crowd pays $100 a day in season for a cottage with its own beach, meals included, this off-season family of six easily bargained its way to the same accommodations — without meals — for a mere $120 a month.

When the millionaires are playing elsewhere

A resort owner who has to keep his place open anyway can use your dollars. He doesn't really care about your social status or income, especially when his millionaires are playing elsewhere.

Think the way the rich do, and get results. The wealthy man books ahead, makes and gets confirmed reservations, pays for a night's stay in advance or makes a deposit. He's never ignored by a headwaiter, snubbed by a room clerk, or seated next to the kitchen. You won't be either if you write, in advance, state the time you are coming, what you require, and for how long. Ask for confirmed reservations, and enclose a stamped self-addressed envelope. Arm yourself with a few first-rate credit cards and use your membership number when making reservations.

This way you will get a nod and a smile from the headwaiter when he finds your name on his list. He will take you to your reserved table by the window while others wait behind a velvet rope.

Get acquainted with telephone numbers that begin with 800. These are the toll-free systems that reserve rooms, tickets, car rentals everywhere in the world.

The telephone operator can help, or you can check the yellow pages for the numbers used by chain companies, or call a local branch of the chain and your request will be taken care of. If you're using a pay phone, you'll even get your dime back.

Aim for the best: travelers who strive to save money by settling for the mediocre often get a poor bargain. The least expensive meal on the menu of a fine restaurant will share the chef's skill, the service, and the pleasant surroundings of the higher-priced meals. Yet it will usually cost less than the top dinner in a cheap restaurant where preparation, skill and surroundings are far inferior.

For the ultimate in a touch of mink travel, rent it. Rent a Rolls Royce for an evening at the theater. Rent a mink coat, or even jewels.

It's nice to know you don't have to make the payments on a Rolls to ride in one, or pay the insurance on furs and jewels. Many millionaires and movie stars have discovered it can be more satisfactory to rent than to pack along their own luxuries and worry about thieves and insurance. Any ordinary family can use these same techniques. Reserve ahead, plan ahead, enjoy the best. Take the time to consult lists of gourmet eating establishments and best-places-to-stay, listed in paperback guides and magazines.

CHAPTER XIII

Taking the Kids — and Surviving

Elsewhere we have a number of times touched on the subject of vacationing with children. In this chapter we will examine the degree of truth in Robert Benchley's quip that there are two kinds of travel — first class and with children.

Admittedly, children under 5 need a lot of care and benefit little from exotic scenery. And youngsters in their teens can make problems wherever they are, including right at home. But many segments of the travel industry are trying to take the pain out and putting pleasure back in by offering nursery facilities, teen-centers, and meals designed for children plus recreation for children on trains, planes, ships, buses and at campgrounds.

Many hotels and motels now offer baby-sitting services, free baby beds and high chairs; some even encourage you to bring sleeping bags and bed the whole family in one room if your budget calls for that economy.

Some families save money and keep the children in what may be a more natural element for them by camping. For those who prefer to take their comforts along in their own recreational vehicles, there's a new kind of home away from home. It's variously called a camptel (for camp-hotel) Venture Out, Camp Inn, Travel Park, Trav-L-Park, Outside Inn, Safari Camp, or even a Yogi Bear Jellystone Park. Already there are hundreds along major highways and scenic areas. The outlook is for many more soon, from coast-to-coast, with most major motel chains and oil companies getting into the act.

Facilities are aimed at families with children. If you arrive in a car without camping equipment, you may be able to rent a tent, mobile home, or even a Conestoga wagon.

A list of camptel facilities may include any or all of these and more: heated swimming pool, mini-golf, bicycle rentals, pony rides, cartoon movie theater, guided tours, a "teen hut," billiards, horseshoe pitching, craft lessons, a well-stocked store, laundry facilities, hot showers, hair-care center, baby-sitting service. One has a tree designated for initial-carving.

Well operated, immaculate, supervised camping hotels usually charge between $2 and $6 a night for a family of any size.

Traveling with children, according to Robert Benchley,
is one of two ways to go. The other one is first class.

Some have a cross-country toll-free reservation system. You can drive across the country, reserving ahead, knowing you won't have to cope with a bunch of tired children and a "No Vacancy" sign at the end of the day's drive.

Camp stops such as these keep children from becoming bored off the road but they'll be better on-the-road travelers if you give them something to do.

Each youngster should have a share of responsibility in planning and executing a successful trip. Give them some real jobs.

Let one take over the task of seeing that all the luggage is packed scientifically each day, no cinch in a crowded station wagon or on a car rack.

A teenager is capable of keeping an itemized record of daily expenditures, of seeing that spending is kept within bounds of the budget, of distributing allowances.

One family avoided all freeway travel in its cross-country vacation, thanks to a son who introduced them to "shunpiking." He acquired maps and planned the route on little-known roads through scenic and historic small towns where traffic was light.

Map reading and navigating are teenage jobs in our family, with admittedly mixed results. Kay, our daughter who prides herself on being an expert highway guide, once overlooked the fact that Highway 30S was not 30N and took us down a narrow road from which, with two tons of trailer behind, there was no turning back. So we kept right on going west on the wrong highway — for miles and miles.

No harm done, though, and we learned that it's essential to hang loose when you travel, and not get upset by change of plan or road.

In another traveling family, the college-freshman daughter contributed knowledge gained in courses on Renaissance art and medieval culture to guide her family to exhibits and churches they'd never have known about had they toured Italy without her.

A 5-year-old can be entrusted with the job of seeing that windshield and mirrors are clean for each start.

Travel is a mind-expanding experience, too, when it's permitted to be. Children automatically absorb lessons in geography, history, ecology. They learn to work purposefully with math when they must budget an allowance or, in foreign travel, learn how to convert dollars and cents into other currencies. They taste new foods, meet new people.

They do all these things with amazing skill and aplomb, as evidenced by our six- and eight-year-old daughters' bargaining session to obtain burro rides at their price (ten pesos an hour — all of 80 cents from a Mexican farmer. The girls didn't speak Spanish, at least at the beginning, nor did the farmer speak English, but sign language and smiles and quickly learned vocabulary did the job.

Both to make children fit to travel with and to make

the travel valuable for them, considerable advance filling-in is essential. It's all too easy to assume a knowledge of geography that few children have when it comes to places outside their own neighborhood.

We set out once to drive from where we were then living, near New York City, to Cedar Rapids, Iowa. We'd built up the goal of the trip magnificently: "We're going to see Grandma again but this time we'll see Grandpa, too, and we'll visit at their house and play with their animals" and so on and on.

But evidently we'd neglected the geography. As we drove through Bear Mountain Park, our cross-country trip less than an hour old, our kindergartner demanded, "Are we in Cedar Rapids?"

Just as young children can be social disasters on some occasions, they can be social assets on others. Ours have initiated valuable friend-ships for the whole family more than once, most notably on our first venture out of the American continent.

Two of our girls, then 7 and 9, returned from an exciting session of riding the ship's elevator up and down aboard the Dutch liner *Statendam*, Europe-bound, to tell us about a new friend of their own age.

"We think you should come and meet her parents, too," said one of the girls.

That's how we met Ed and Bee Boettiger, whom we liked so much we camped with them in Spain and

Morocco the next year and with whom, many years later, we went around the world (still camping, whenever possible).

To hold a youngster's interest, the adventure of a vacation should begin weeks, months before your departure date. It takes time to acquire maps, guidebooks, sightseeing literature, transportation schedules, reservations. Older youngsters can handle the bulk of this job and enjoy receiving travel mail in their own names to pass on to the others.

Preceding a major trip by making a trial run is good sense, especially if you're planning some drastic innovation, like camping for the first time. And make a list of gadgets, devices and small travel conveniences you will need.

If you don't find it easy to reconcile yourself to travel *with* children, consider the disadvantages of traveling *without* them.

You'll be worrying about what's going on back home, running up astronomical phone bills, and losing out on the bonuses that come with having them along. Without children to escort you, in fact, you might miss out on a lot of these delights:
• A tour of toy shops; a visit to a museum that has a doll collection; puppet shows; collecting items that convert into toys (pine cones, driftwood, stones, shells); a visit to a toymaker; buying miniature doll furniture; a cable-car trip in ski country (rides avail-

able in the summer, too); holiday celebrations geared to children's interests (Thanksgiving Day parades in New York and San Francisco); a visit to Disneyland in California, Disney World in Florida; miniature train rides; pony parks, zoos, animal exhibits such as Zumstein's Reindeer Ranch, just west of Redmond, Oregon (free), animal parks featuring wild animals in natural settings: Lion Country Safari in California, Tampa African Complex in Florida, Warner Brothers Jungle Habitat in New Jersey and, in the near future, the Living World of Ringling Brothers in Florida.

On a trip children can help you broaden your horizons in the course of broadening their own.

CHAPTER XIV

Souvenirs: To Buy or Not To Buy

Thoughtlessly acquired souvenirs can knock quite a hole in an otherwise sound vacation budget, leaving you only with shelves burdened with dust-catchers. The time to prevent this kind of money leak is before you leave home. How? By reaching a family agreement on principles.

Children are rarely aware of any limits on family funds, so allot a personal-and-souvenir allowance for each person according to age and needs. Teenagers can acquire money know-how by getting their entire vacation fund in the form of travelers checks at the start of the trip, while younger children may need to have their funds doled out daily or weekly.

Large purchases for the house — furniture, rugs, paintings, what not — should be discussed before being bought. Shun impulse buying. Is the thing really needed? Would it be purchased anyway during the coming year? How does it fit in with the things you now own? Can the cost be spread over several months? Is the store a reputable one? (Consult a Better Business Bureau in the area if your purchase is a large one.)

Paintings can often be purchased with a credit card. Some artists will rent a painting and refund the rental fee if the work is purchased later, a safeguard against bad judgment and impulse buying.

Look at souvenirs as falling into three general classes: the free ones; the inexpensive purchases; and those of major impact on the household and its budget.

Free souvenirs are the things you collect by looking, and they can be the best of all. A walk on a beach produces a pocketful of interesting stones or shells. In some areas, mountain as well as seashore, there are tons of driftwood from which to select a rare piece. Indeed, mountain driftwood, shaped by the wind, is often more dramatic than the shapes produced by water.

Some beaches yield valuable agate, jade, fossils, gems. Go armed with a paperback nature guide — you can find inexpensive ones for each type of collecting — telling you what to look for and where to look. If you get that guidebook before you go and let a youngster do some advance planning, you may hear him take charge: "Hey, we're getting close to Big Sur. Jade Beach is right near here. Let's see what we can find."

He will already know that this beach, the scene of valuable finds, is not too well known, and is a place where a casual visitor can expect to pick up fine (but small) California jade stones with no difficulty.

Pine cones, easily found, can become Christmas wreaths and candle holders. A stone can be polished and used for a paperweight. Driftwood makes a good

Beaches are for more than sunbathing: some yield objects
of value to the knowing comber: jade, agate, fossils, whatnots.

planter. Our home has a few doorknobs and drawer handles made from smoothed chunks of driftwood collected at beaches by our children.

Souvenirs of this kind can become small but rather meaningful Christmas gifts, too, and thus help the holiday budget.

Collecting begun on a vacation trip can turn into a lifetime hobby, a scientific career or a profitable business venture.

One tourist began painting amusing faces on a few stones she had picked up at the beach. Friends admired them — and now you can buy them in gift and stationery stores throughout the country.

More commercial, but still free, are such collectible souvenirs as menus, napkins, free maps of towns and parks. These can be turned into wall or table-top collages rather than end up in a drawer. Match books are another free collectible.

The most interesting Christmas tree in our town must surely be the one displayed by the Gilmore family. From the time of their marriage, on every trip they took, Don and Edith bought only tiny items, originally to conserve space in their midget car. They began with a pair of Katchina dolls, a souvenir of their honeymoon in Indian country.

After children came along, the tree sprouted with their own travel choices: tiny toy instruments, minia- ture flags, small carved animals, handmade jewelry, and tiny baskets. Each item on the tree has a story, a memory, and many bear the name of the place where they were acquired.

Inexpensive postcards and color slides make a good trip record. Really attractive postcards are worth collecting to send out as greeting cards even long after they've been brought home.

To keep expenditures in line, don't throw your buymanship know-how to the winds just because you're vacationing. Avoid when possible stores that are strictly tourist oriented. In a resort town there will always be drug and dry-goods stores that cater to the local folk and offer much of the same merchandise without marked-up tourist prices. Look for the point of origin mark on every item. You don't want to find to your later chagrin that you've toted home a scarf made in Hong Kong — unless, of course it was Hong Kong you bought it in.

Watch for genuine sales. Toward season's end local merchants everywhere mark down regular merchandise. Sales are fun, especially in cities or countries far from home. We've enjoyed competing for bargains when we happened to arrive in Copenhagen just as the August *udsalg* started.

Something you really need or can well use in your home may cost no more and mean far more to you if bought as a part of a memorable vacation.

Knowing what is a good buy where can make a vacation
a profitable experience as well as a pleasant one.

A Navajo rug of good quality, handwoven in the
ancient fashion, is more of an investment these days
than a casual purchase. You might decide to buy one
in a trustworthy shop in New Mexico.

You may have been planning to buy a certain piece
of furniture. It makes sense to get it from a craftsman
who, let's say, makes each piece individually and
uniquely in a Mexican village — but only if the item is
really what you want.

Travel purchases, especially handcrafted ones, are
frequently one-of-a-kind items. This applies to paint-

ings, sculpture, antiques, jewelry, some furniture. Remember when dealing with the unique that although hasty buying is risky, so is passing up something you really want in the hope you'll find the same item cheaper in the next town. You'll probably never see its like again.

Some hunches are worth playing. You might be as lucky as a Kansas friend of ours who audibly admired a garnet necklace in a little shop in Berlin. The price was about $31. Her husband slipped back a few hours later to buy it and gave it to her back home the next Christmas, in 1958.

In 1972 she took it to a jeweler for a small repair on the clasp. He offered to buy the necklace for $300, admitting it was probably worth much more. The necklace was not for sale, of course; it's now on the way to becoming a family heirloom with a history.

Souvenirs that don't dent the budget

Clothing that is really needed can have souvenir value without harm to the budget. Indeed, handmade clothing or garments purchased directly from a factory in an area you are visiting may be a bargain in price or of better quality than you could buy at home.

On a trip to Scotland we acquired brand-name cashmere cardigans for ourselves and for gifts for only $10 apiece at a mill store. Though the sweaters are seconds, their flaws are almost invisible. If you visit Helsinki, Finland, you'll find you can buy seconds of the world-famous expensive Arabia china at low prices.

Warning: Don't purchase a local "costume" garment unless you really want, well, a costume. A squaw dress, a dirndl, a thick Scottish tweed suit is fine in the area where it's made but a dead loss if you'd be embarrassed, or smothered, if you wore it in your own hometown.

You can usually have a purchase mailed directly home at no extra cost except postage; this saves you the trouble of carrying or wrapping it yourself. Some shops will take your gift list and mail items to your friends at dates you specify, enclosing gift cards you sign. When shopping abroad, you should know that any gift $10 or under, retail price, can be mailed home without payment of duty. But anything you carry home with you will count as part of your $100 duty-exempt allowance.

The relative or friend to shun

Things can get very much out of hand if you let yourself feel obligated to buy a gift for everyone you know just because you're traveling. And you are entitled to shun the relative or friend who seeks to make your vacation an excuse for having his personal shopping done in some distant spot. The responsibility of doing his errands can be as objectionable as the nuisance, since purchases made at distant points are difficult to exchange or return for refund.

Buy only things that please you and are kind to your purse. For those of your friends whom you wish to remember, give a we've-come-home party and let them see what you've brought. Let each choose something he likes. What remains unchosen will still be things you want yourself. Feelings and cash are both spared.

CHAPTER XV

Keeping in Touch

Great as it is to get away from the everyday routine, you'll probably want or need to keep in touch with home, at least to the extent of being quickly reachable in an emergency.

If your trip has a scheduled itinerary, this is easy. Just leave with your informal or formal caretaker a list of where you'll be and when and how you can be reached at each place by mail, cable or phone. Note time-zone differences if any are involved.

Mail to be sent to you in care of your hotel, motel, park or recreation-area office should be marked "Hold for arrival" or "Return to sender after . . ." a specified date.

Any US Post Office will hold mail addressed to you in care of General Delivery. Traveling abroad? In most countries it's called Poste Restante.

If you're getting mail in a foreign country, advise correspondents to print name and address clearly. It's a good idea to have them put your last name in capital letters.

For one thing, you'll avoid the experience of the traveling Briton who didn't receive a series of important letters. Addressed to "Harry Jones, Esquire," they were regularly pigeonholed under "E." Likewise, in a country where the family name comes in the middle, mail addressed to Edgar Allan Poe might languish under "A" forever unless "Poe" were capitalized or underlined.

In arranging to receive mail by General Delivery in the US, remember that post offices close on weekends and holidays. With the new prevalence of Monday holidays this could cost you a three-day delay.

Special delivery is another potential trap. In a rural area, if you're not around when the mailman comes, your special delivery letter goes back to the post office with him. You may be days in catching up with it.

So unless you warn correspondents about this, your very most important mail may, ironically, take longest to reach you.

Registered mail can create similar problems, anywhere you go. A daughter just back from a period of rural life on a Greek island tells of missing the mail mule one day when there was a registered letter for her, of having to trudge three kilometers to the village, then wait hours for postman and mule to return from the mountains.

Here are a number of alternate mail drops for regular or emergency use: worldwide travel companies; a branch of your own bank, or any bank, for that matter; any automobile club office in the US or abroad (whether you're a member or not); any embassy or consulate of the US when you're abroad; the personal address of a friend or (with permission) the friend of a friend.

Heavy correspondence obligations can dent a vacation budget. Save money on postage by using regular mail, rather than air, whenever possible. Most mail in the US goes by air anyway. To countries outside this hemisphere, and from most of them, you can use aerograms: lower postage costs, no stationery necessary.

Save time and effort by carrying a supply of stamped postcards and stamped envelopes. Use the "chain" letter system: conclude each major letter with a list of names and addresses of people to whom it is to be passed along. If you add your own name at the end, your letters will automatically become a diary of your vacation.

Equally simple strategies cut phoning costs way down, too.

Use the new dial-it-yourself, one-minute phone call, now available anywhere in the US from 11 p.m. to 8 a.m. for not more than 35 cents. But it's economical only if you hold down your phone time, so think out your message in advance and don't linger.

Before you leave, get a telephone credit card. This can save you money by giving you a record of business calls that are tax deductible or chargeable to an expense account. And you won't have to fumble for change to use in a phone booth.

Let it be known that you will be reachable daily through one friend or relative. By prearrangement call that person at a specified time each day. The understanding is he'll answer the phone at that minute only if he has a message or other reason to talk to you.

One minor disaster that often happens to travelers is getting separated in a large city without a clearly agreed upon place to meet. Once we agreed by mail with some very old friends in Iowa that our group of six would join the four of them for a vacation in Guadalajara, Mexico. The first family to arrive would leave a message for the other at American Express, we suggested — surely there must be one there. Fine, our Iowa friends wrote back, but if there's any hitch about Amexco, leave word at the YWCA instead. We *know* there's one of those because a friend of ours used to work in it. We replied by adding a third possibility. "If all else fails, meet us at the American Library at high noon on Wednesday. We're definitely told there is one."

So what came of all this careful planning?

Neither the phone book nor anyone we or our friends asked had heard of American Express. (The company is represented there, but not under its own name.)

The YWCA? Well, it was there, all right — or so we were told much later. But it didn't occur to us that the name, and hence the initials, had to be quite different in Spanish. So naturally neither inquiries nor search of two phone books (yes, two — there turned out to be two competing telephone companies) gave us any clue.

As it happens, we found the American Library, though with some difficulty and after being told many times that it did not exist. Since it was hiding under the name of Bibliotecas Benjamin Franklin (and you'd better pronounce that Ben-ha-meen Frahnk-leen) our friends failed to uncover it.

Only chance saved us from further frustration. On the evening of our second day in the city, while shopping in a boutique, we were hailed by a fellow-Yank.

"You by any chance the Californians with the four blonde daughters" — he pointed at them — "that a fellow named Hank Felson has everybody in town looking for?"

CHAPTER XVI

Your Home, Your Insurance and Yourself

For a carefree vacation, re-examine your insurance policies before you leave. Read the fine print and discuss all applicable provisions with your insurance agent or broker.

Even an honestly written policy, perfectly adequate under everyday conditions, may need changes or additions to protect a house that's vacant or one temporarily occupied by a sitter or handyman. People and possessions on the move may require different coverage than when stationary.

If your household policy was taken out some years ago, it may be overdue for an increase in face amount

Do you have insurance protection against whatever ills may befall? Health? Lost luggage? Theft? Fire (back home)?

to take care of the value added by the last few years of inflation or recent improvements.

Your problem is simplified if the policy on your house is of the type called homeowners. This kind generally covers not only your house but appurtenant structures (a playhouse, tool house, woodshed), furnishings, personal property you take with you on vacation, temporary living expenses if your house is damaged beyond use, and personal liability plus medical payments to others who may use or care for the house in your absence.

Make sure your policy remains fully effective even when the house is unoccupied. Owners of an estate near Cold Spring, NY, not only rented us a mansion filled with antiques but threw in, for the $30 a month rent, the free services of a part-time handyman just to keep their insurance policies effective while they were on an extended vacation.

Our own homeowners policy, for example, will pay up to $8,250 on our personal property, probably not enough now since it covers furnishings plus loss to any property we carry with us anywhere in the world. On one extended tour our car was ransacked. A tent was destroyed by a storm in Sicily. A small electrical fire at home damaged a hallway and rug. We were reimbursed adequately. However, if all of our furnishings had been destroyed, too, we'd have taken quite a loss.

Before you go, make an itemized list of possessions and their value. A photograph of anything unique or especially valuable, such as a sculpture or painting, is helpful in making a claim if the object is destroyed or stolen. It's a good idea to make another list of things you're taking along.

Borrow a marking device, free from most police departments or your insurance agent, to identify valuables by etching on them your Social Security number or car license. Keep a record of serial numbers of mechanical possessions. Leave lists, policies and personal papers with your bank or lawyer, not in the house itself.

Someone — a neighbor or handyman — coming to check the place daily is a form of insurance, too. An unoccupied house is in more danger from vandalism, burglary, or internal unnoticed damage (a broken waterline, a leak in a hot-water tank, a short-circuit) than one which is occupied.

The Nelsons found this out. Their house was so thoroughly locked up that a faulty hot-water tank had time to pour boiling water on rugs and hardwood floors for hours before a neighbor observed that the windows were steamed up — in midsummer.

This incident points to one good reason for leaving a key with a neighbor or friend who can make a quick check — preferably daily. An alternative or supplementary precaution is an arrangement with the police department to check your house regularly to try door locks and shine a light into the interior.

If you acquire several inexpensive timers, lights and radios can go on and off at intervals in a most convincing way. There's even a type that will start any gadget at whatever time you set it for — and then turn it off at different times each night. This can fool even a sophisticated "caser" who would spot any-

A house left dark night after night signals the burglar
that you are away and the house is burglarable.

thing that switches on and off at the same hour daily.

The controlled light should preferably be in a bath-room or some other interior spot where no one out-side can determine if the room is occupied. A radio left at low volume is at least equally effective.

A place of your own, where you regularly vacation — for example, a cottage you occupy only a few weeks a year — is a tempting target for damage from weather, vandals, even from visitors to whom you may rent or lend it. Your insurance should be for all year, not for just the pleasant summer days when you're there.

Are there special hazards — forest fires, streams that flood in spring, heavy snowfall, hurricanes, tornadoes? If so, are you covered?

Consider saving some premium costs by choosing a policy with a deductible clause. Minor damages you can repair or replace with your own labor. Only total loss would be a real hardship.

Reduce fire hazards by cutting nearby brush. Check and repair, if necessary, the roof, shut off all utilities, store clothing and food in metal containers, remove valuables.

Insurance should protect that occasional well-meaning visitor, too. A neighbor or watchman could trip on the loose porch step or fall over a worn rug. Personal liability and medical payments could save you a lawsuit.

The next insurance policy to check, after the one on your home (or homes), is car insurance. Do you carry enough? Most people think they do. Nevertheless, because requirements differ, liability insurance which meets your own state laws might get you into a lot of trouble in another state where you're vacationing.

As a resident of Louisiana, let's say, you carry $5,000 property damage, $10,000 for injury to a person. This meets the state law. But on your vacation you drive to northern Michigan and have an accident. You're in serious trouble, because here the law requires $10,000 property damage, $20,000 bodily injury payments on each person. Get in an accident in some states and

With the right insurance on your house, you can leave it with a clear conscience to go lallygagging.

you could end up in jail, have your license revoked at the scene of the accident, have your car impounded, or be required to put up a large cash bond or immediate proof of financial responsibility.

If you drive across the border to Mexico you might have the misfortune to kill a cow. This is easy in a country where many areas are unfenced and animals wander the highways. Nevertheless, killing an animal could get you in heavy trouble unless you carry Mexican insurance. Your US policy is invalid. Special Mexican coverage is available at the border. It's expensive, but it's one risk you can't afford to take.

Canada, our other close border, honors US insurance policies, but here again your coverage might be inadequate. Some areas of Canada require you to carry $50,000 liability coverage.

Going camping? If you're towing a trailer, driving a camper, hauling a motorcycle or a couple of bikes, carrying a boat on top, you're loaded with hazards. Chances are you don't have coverage for these extras, yet you're carrying an unusually heavy load and driving under difficult conditions. Why risk it without insurance?

You can obtain specific information on driving conditions and insurance laws in other areas through your auto club or write directly to the motor vehicles departments in state capitals.

For medical insurance on yourself, Blue Cross and Blue Shield policies are good anywhere in the world. If you pay a medical bill yourself in a hospital that doesn't honor these policies, keep the receipts, and present them to your own health insurance office for reimbursement as soon as you return home.

Many other health insurance plans are void if you go out of the United States. You may need to take out a special short-term policy for the area in which you're vacationing.

Read your policies. Will all members of your family be covered? On public transportation? If you rent a car? Are there special exclusions? If someone has a major accident or illness would the policy pay ambulance or air-stretcher costs back to your home?

If you vacation abroad you may discover that a nationalized medical program in the country you are visiting will care for your family without charge, or at low cost, in an emergency illness.

Surgery for one of us in Copenhagen cost $5 a day for complete hospital care. The services of the surgeon were free. An ulcerated tooth was removed by a dentist in an English village. The fee was $2.80.

Two young hitch-hikers from New Jersey, seriously injured in a car accident in Austria, reported excellent care in a hospital there. The day they were released they were told, "You have suffered so much, and your pain spoiled your vacation. We do not wish to give you a bill." The boys had grateful and well off parents who insisted on paying. And they had to insist.

Flight insurance is looked into in detail elsewhere in this series. Basically, it's not a good buy, according to the odds.

Another type of vacation insurance is the one that pays off if your vacation is rained out. Here again the insurance company isn't losing money. This type of protection is usually offered only where the average vacation season, summer, is rarely rainy. And it's safe to assume you can buy no such insurance if you plan to camp in the Northwest rain forest.

Transportation companies advertise that your ticket includes insurance on your luggage. True, but the coverage is limited. Often it amounts to $500 total or to $100 per suitcase, which in your case might be quite inadequate.

If you're carrying several complete outfits, shoes, a camera, jewelry and souvenirs, you'd probably be out many dollars if your luggage were destroyed or disappeared. But if you have a homeowners policy, you may already be insured on loss of personal possessions, so why double up by taking another policy?

Actually, although airlines lose about 2% of all luggage, most of it is merely missent and shows up in a few days. Insure yourself against the inconvenience caused by missent suitcases by carrying one piece of hand luggage with essentials (medicine, valuables, passport, travelers checks, toiletries, cosmetics, a light change of clothing) and keeping it with you at all times. Your airline might pay for immediate essentials you might have to buy if your luggage is lost for several days.

APPENDIX

US Governmental Sources of US Tourist Information

The US Travel Service sends to foreigners asking for information this list of state and territorial offices which provide brochures, maps, etc. You don't *have* to be a foreigner to get the materials.

Alabama
Bureau of Publicity and
    Information
State Highway Building
Montgomery, AL 36104

Alaska
Travel Div.
Pouc E
Juneau, AK 99801

Arizona
Travel Development Section
3003 North Central Av.,
    Suite 1704
Phoenix, AZ 85012

Arkansas
Dept. of Parks and
    Tourism
149 State Capitol Building
Little Rock, AR 72201

California
Div. of Tourism and
    Visitor Services
1400 Tenth St.
Sacramento, CA 95814

Canal Zone
Panama Canal Co.
425 13 St. NW
Washington, DC 20004

Colorado
Travel Marketing Section
602 State Capitol Annex
Denver, CO 80203

Connecticut
Development Comm.
Vacation Travel Promotion
210 Washington St.
Hartford, CT 06115

Delaware
Bureau of Travel
    Development
Dept. of Community
    Affairs
45 The Green
Dover, DE 19901

**District of Columbia
    (Washington, DC)**
Convention and Visitors
    Bureau
1129 20th St., NW
Washington, DC 20036

Florida
Div. of Tourism
107 West Gaines St.
Tallahassee, FL 32304

Georgia
Tourist Div.
PO Box 38097
Atlanta, GA 30334

Guam
Visitors Bureau
PO Box 3520
Agana, GU 96910

Hawaii
Visitors Bureau
2270 Kalakaua Av.
    Suite 801
Honolulu, HI 96815

Idaho
Dept. of Commerce and
    Development
State Capitol Building
    Rm. 108
Boise, ID 83707

Illinois
Div. of Tourism
222 South College St.
Springfield, IL 62706

Indiana
Div. of Tourism
State House, Rm. 336
Indianapolis, IN 46204

Iowa
Development Comm.
Tourism and Travel
    Div.
250 Jewett Building
Des Moines, IA 50309

Kansas
Travel Div.
122-S State Office Building
Topeka, KS 66612

Kentucky
Advertising and Travel
    Promotion
Capitol Annex Building
Frankfort, KY 40601

Louisiana
Tourist Development
    Comm.
PO Box 44291
Baton Rouge, LA 70804

Maine
Promotion Div.
Dept. of Commerce and
    Industry
State House
Augusta, ME 04330

Maryland
Div. of Tourism
2525 Riva Rd.
Annapolis, MD 21401

Massachusetts
Div. of Tourism
100 Cambridge St.
Boston, MA 02202

Michigan
Tourist Council
300 South Capitol Av.
Suite 102
Lansing, MI 48926

Minnesota
Vacation Information Center
51 East 8th St.
St. Paul, MN 55101

Mississippi
Travel and Tourist
    Dept.
PO Box 849
Rm. 1504
    State Office Building
Jackson, MS 39205

Missouri
Tourism Comm.
PO Box 1055
Jefferson City, MO 65101

Montana
Advertising Unit
Montana Dept. of Highways
Helena, MT 59601

Nebraska
Div. of Travel and
    Tourism
PO Box 94666
Lincoln, NE 68509

Nevada
Tourism-Travel Div.
Carson City, NV 89701

New Hampshire
Div. of Economic
    Development
PO Box 856
Concord, NH 03301

New Jersey
New Jersey State Promotion
PO Box 400
Trenton, NJ 08625

New Mexico
Tourist Div.
113 Washington Av.
Santa Fe, NM 87501

New York
Travel Bureau
112 State St.
Albany, NY 12207

North Carolina
Dept. of Natural and
    Economic Resources
Travel and Promotion
    Div.
PO Box 27687
Raleigh, NC 27611

North Dakota
North Dakota Travel
    Dept.
State Capitol Grounds
Bismarck, ND 58501

Ohio
Travel and Tourist Bureau
PO Box 1001
Columbus, OH 43216

Oklahoma
Publicity and Information
    Div.
Oklahoma Dept. of
    Tourism and Recreation
500 Will Rogers Memorial
    Building
Oklahoma City, OK 73105

Oregon
Travel Information Section
Oregon State Highway
    Div.
Salem, OR 97310

Pennsylvania
Bureau of Travel
    Development
402 South Office Building
Harrisburg, PA 17120

Puerto Rico
Puerto Rico Tourism
    Development Co.
GPO Box BN
San Juan, PR 00936

Rhode Island
Tourist Promotion Div.
Roger Williams Building
Hayes St.
Providence, RI 02908

Samoa
Office of Tourism
Government of American
    Samoa
Pago Pago, AS 96799

South Carolina
Div. of Travel and
    Tourism
Box 1358
Columbia, SC 29202

South Dakota
Travel Div.
South Dakota Dept.
    of Highways
Pierre, SD 57501

Tennessee
Dept. of Economic and
    Community Development
2611 West End Av.
Nashville, TN 37203

Texas
Tourist Development Agency
Box 12008, Capitol Station
Austin, TX 78711

**Trust Territory of
    Pacific Islands**
(Caroline Islands, Mariana
    Islands, Marshall Islands)
Office of Tourism/
    Economic Development
Saipan,
    Mariana Islands 96950

Utah
Travel Council
Council Hall, Capitol Hill
Salt Lake City, UT 84114

Vermont
Information/Travel
    Development Div.
61 Elm St.
Montpelier, VT 05602

Virgin Islands
Tourist Bureau
PO Box 1692
Charlotte Amalie
St. Thomas, VI 00801

Virginia
State Travel Service
911 East Broad St.
Richmond, VA 23219

Washington
Tourist Development
    Div.
General Administration
    Building
Olympia, WA 98504

West Virginia
Travel Development
    Div.
1900 Washington St.
Charleston, WV 25305

Wisconsin
Bureau of Vacation and
    Travel Services
Box 450
Madison, WI 53701

Wyoming
Travel Comm.
2320 Capitol Av.
Cheyenne, WY 82001

US State Parks

Here are addresses which will help you obtain information on public parks maintained by states.

Alabama
Div. of State Parks
Montgomery 36104

Alaska
Parks & Recreation Section
323 East Fourth Av.
Anchorage 99501

Arizona
State Parks
1611 West Adams St.
Phoenix 85007

Arkansas
State Parks
Recreation & Travel Comm.
149 State Capitol
Little Rock 72201

California
Dept. of Parks & Recreation
PO Box 2390
Sacramento 95811

Colorado
Parks & Recreation
Planning
6060 Broadway
Denver 80216

Connecticut
State Park & Forest Comm.
165 Capitol Av.
Hartford 06115

Delaware
Dept. of Natural Resources
& Environmental Control
Dover 19901

Florida
Div. of Recreation & Parks
101 West Gaines St.
Tallahassee 32301

Georgia
Dept. of State Parks
270 Washington St., SW
Atlanta 30334

Hawaii
Div. of State Parks
PO Box 621
Honolulu 96809

Idaho
Dept. of Parks
Capitol Building
Boise 83702

Illinois
Div. of Parks & Memorials
113 State Office Building
Springfield 62706

Indiana
Div. of State Parks
State Office Building
Indianapolis 46209

Iowa
State Conservation Comm.
300 Fourth St.
Des Moines 50319

Kansas
State Park & Resources
Authority
801 Harrison
Topeka 66612

Kentucky
Dept. of Parks
Capitol Annex
Frankfort 40601

Louisiana
State Parks & Recreation
Comm.
PO Box 1111
Baton Rouge 70821

Maine
State Park & Recreation
Comm.
State House
Augusta 04330

Maryland
Dept. of State Forests
& Parks
State Office Building
Annapolis 21401

Massachusetts
Div. of Forests & Parks
100 Cambridge St.
Boston 02108

Michigan
Parks Div.
Stevens T. Mason Building
Lansing 48926

Minnesota
Div. of State Parks
& Recreation
Centennial Building
St. Paul 55101

Mississippi
State Park Comm.
717 Robert E. Lee Building
Jackson 39201

Missouri
State Park Board
PO Box 176
Jefferson City 65101
Ozark Playgrounds Assoc.
212 West Fourth
Joplin 64801

Montana
Div. of State Parks
Helena 59601

Nebraska
Game & Parks Comm.
Lincoln 68509

Nevada
State Park System
201 South Fall St.
Carson City 89701

New Hampshire
Div. of Parks
State House Annex
Concord 03301

New Jersey
Bureau of Parks
PO Box 1420
Trenton 08625

New Mexico
State Park & Recreation
Comm.
PO Box 1147
Santa Fe 87501

New York
State Parks & Recreation
Albany 12226
Council of Parks
380 Madison Av.
New York 10017

North Carolina
Div. of State Parks
PO Box 27687
Raleigh 27611

North Dakota
North Dakota Park Services
State Office Building
Bismarck 58501

Ohio
Div. of Parks & Recreation
913 Ohio Depts. Building
Columbus 43215

Oklahoma
Industrial Development &
   Park Dept.
500 Will Rogers Memorial
   Building
Oklahoma City 73105

Oregon
State Parks Div.
State Highway Dept.
Salem 97310

Pennsylvania
Bureau of State Parks
PO Box 1467
Harrisburg 17126

Rhode Island
Div. of Parks & Recreation
83 Park St.
Providence 02903

South Carolina
Dept. of Parks, Recreation
   & Tourism
PO Box 1358
Columbia 29202

South Dakota
Div. of Parks & Recreation
Pierre 57501

Tennessee
Div. of State Parks
2611 West End Av.
Nashville 37203

Texas
Parks Information
John Reagan Building
Austin 78701

Utah
State Park & Recreation
   Comm.
132 South 2nd West
Salt Lake City 84101

Vermont
Dept. of Forests & Parks
Montpelier 05601

Virginia
Div. of Parks
7th and Main St.
Richmond 23219

Washington
State Parks & Recreation
   Comm.
PO Box 1128
Olympia 98501

West Virginia
Div. of Parks & Recreation
Charleston 25305

Wisconsin
Recreation Commission
PO Box 309
Cheyenne 82001

US National Parks and
Other National Park Service facilities

Below are listed the names and addresses of the National Parks of
the US. For information on other facilities administered by the
National Park Service, write to Superintendent of Documents,
Government Printing Office, Washington, DC 20402 for Price List
35, which tells what brochures are available and their prices.

Arcadia National Park
Hulls Cove, Maine 04644

Big Bend National Park
Big Bend, Texas 79834

Bryce Canyon, National Park
Bryce Canyon, Utah 84717

Canyonlands National Park
Moab, Utah 84532

Carlsbad Caverns National
   Park
Carlsbad, New Mexico 88220

Crater Lake National Park
Crater Lake, Oregon 97604

Everglades National Park
Homestead, Florida 33030

Glacier National Park
West Glacier, Montana 59936

Grand Canyon National Park
Grand Canyon, Arizona
   86023

Grand Teton National Park
Moose, Wyoming 83012

Great Smoky Mountains
   National Park
Gatlinburg, Tennessee 37738

Guadalupe Mountains
   National Park, Texas
   c/o Carlsbad Caverns
   National Park, Carlsbad,
   New Mexico 88220

Haleakala National Park
Kahului, Maui, Hawaii 96732

Hawaii Volcanoes National
   Park
Hawaii 96718

Hot Springs National Park
Hot Springs, Arkansas 71901

Isle Royale National Park
Houghton, Michigan 49931

Kings Canyon National Park
Three Rivers, California
   93271

Lassen Volcanic National
   Park
Mineral, California 96063

Mammoth Cave National
   Park
Mammoth Cave, Kentucky

Mesa Verde National Park
Mesa Verde, Colorado 81330

Mount McKinley National Park
Anchorage, Alaska 99755

Mount Rainier National Park
Longmire, Washington 98397

North Cascades National Park
Sedro Wooley, Washington 98284

Olympic National Park
Port Angeles, Washington 98362

Petrified Forest National Park
Holbrook, Arizona 86025

Platt National Park
Sulphur, Oklahoma 73086

Redwood National Park
Crescent City, California 95531

Rocky Mountain National Park
Estes Park, Colorado 80517

Sequoia National Park
Three Rivers, California 93271

Shenandoah National Park
Luray, Virginia 22835

Virgin Islands National Park
St. Thomas, Virgin Islands 00801

Wind Cave National Park
Hot Springs, South Dakota 57747

Yellowstone National Park
Yellowstone Park, Wyoming 83020

Yosemite National Park
Yosemite Park, California 95389

Zion National Park
Springdale, Utah 84767

For the Traveling History Buff in the US

Here is a compilation and description by the government of historic buildings, sites and museums which can be used to plan a history-oriented vacation.

NEW ENGLAND

MAINE

SEARSPORT: Penobscot Marine Museum of early maritime relics.

YORK VILLAGE: Colonial buildings in their original surroundings include Jefferd's Tavern (1750), furnished as in Revolutionary days, and the Old Gaol (jail), said to be the oldest public building in New England (1653).

PORTLAND: Wadsworth Longfellow House (1785), a Federal period town mansion with personal mementos of the poet.

MASSACHUSETTS

BOSTON: Paul Revere's House (built 1670); Faneuil Hall, the "cradle of liberty"; *USS Constitution*, famous frigate of the War of 1812. Street markers indicate "Freedom Trail," a one-and-a-half-mile walking tour of 15 places of historical interest.

CAMBRIDGE: Harvard College, founded 1636. The oldest building now standing is Massachusetts Hall (1720).

DEERFIELD: This picturesque village was re-built soon after its almost total destruction in an Indian raid in 1704.

SALEM: The House of Seven Gables (1688) was immortalized in Hawthorne's novel.

STURBRIDGE: Old Sturbridge Village, a re-created farming village of the early 1800s, with authentic tools, furniture, and costumes.

SANDWICH (Cape Cod): Site of early glass making industry, many beautiful examples in museum.

PLYMOUTH: Landing place of the Pilgrims in 1620. Several 17th Century houses; a restoration of the original settlement; ship "Mayflower II."

VERMONT

SHELBURNE: Shelburne Museum village of 33 antique buildings with covered bridge and exhibit of folk arts.

BENNINGTON: Museum of Early American glass, costumes and paintings.

PLYMOUTH: Home of President Calvin Coolidge, furnished as it was in 1923 when he was given the Oath of Office by his father, a notary public.

NEW HAMPSHIRE

PLYMOUTH: Museum of original US Patent models showing inventions from 1793 to 1890.

PETERBOROUGH: Goyette Museum of Americana reproduces an early New England street of shops. Authentic antiques and vehicles.

PORTSMOUTH: Some of New England's finest mansions including the Wentworth-Gardner House, an outstanding specimen of Georgian architecture.

RHODE ISLAND

WICKFORD JUNCTION: South County Museum contains large exhibits of Americana, early tools and machinery.

NEWPORT: Old Trinity Church (1726); "The Breakers," palatial mansion of 1895 built by the Vanderbilt family. Touro Synagogue, oldest in the US, (1763).

PROVIDENCE: The State House has many historic paintings and relics on display.

CONNECTICUT

MYSTIC SEAPORT: Reconstruction of an Early American seaport, with an antique whaling ship, a square-rigger, and others. Important nautical museum.

NEW HAVEN: Yale University (1701). The patriot Nathan Hale lived in Connecticut Hall (1752). Winchester Gun Museum traces the history of firearms.

HARTFORD: Old State House (1796) was designed by Thomas Bulfinch.

THE ATLANTIC STATES

NEW YORK

NEW YORK CITY: Statue of Liberty, presented to USA by France, 1884. Circular stairs (168 steps) to interior of head. Fraunces Tavern, where Washington made his farewell address to his officers in 1783; St. Paul's Chapel (1766), oldest public building in NYC.

FORT TICONDEROGA: Built in 1755, once the strategic key to North America, restored.

HYDE PARK: President Franklin and Mrs. Eleanor Roosevelt's home and graves.

WEST POINT: The US Military Academy. Excellent military museum.

TARRYTOWN: Philipsburg Manor (1683), a fortified Dutch manor house and grist mill, period furnished. Old Dutch Church, 1685.

SARATOGA (Bemis Heights): Battlefield (1777) of the Revolutionary War with remains of fortifications, reconstructed blockhouse and powder magazine.

COOPERSTOWN: Farmers' Museum, of buildings, tools, and implements in re-created Early American Village;

Fenimore House contains world's leading collection of American folk arts.

NEW JERSEY

MORRISTOWN: Washington's headquarters in Ford Mansion (1779); rare Washington mementos in historical museum.

PRINCETON: Princeton University; Nassau Hall (1756), where Congress met in 1783.

WEST ORANGE: Library and laboratory of inventor Thomas A. Edison.

PENNSYLVANIA

PHILADELPHIA: Independence Hall, where Declaration of Independence was signed; house where Betsy Ross sewed first US Flag. Christ Church (1727) with grave of Benjamin Franklin.

GETTYSBURG: National Military Park commemorates major Civil War battle (1863). Numerous monuments, tours, museums, weapons and cycloramic exhibits explain the battle.

VALLEY FORGE: Washington's winter headquarters (1777-78). Monuments, museum and reconstructions of the army's huts.

DELAWARE

WILMINGTON: Hagley Yard, museum and restoration of Early American industries; Winterthur Museum; more than 100 rooms of USA architecture, furniture, ceramics, textiles and paintings from 1640 to 1840.

MARYLAND

BALTIMORE: Fort McHenry; the sight of its flag under bombardment in 1814 inspired the writing of the USA's National Anthem "The Star Spangled Banner."

ANNAPOLIS: US Naval Academy, large collection of historic ship models in Naval Museum. Old State House (1772) and numerous other very fine Georgian buildings.

WASHINGTON, DC

WHITE HOUSE: Begun in 1792, painted white after fire during War of 1812 during which President Madison's wife, Dolly, rescued the Gilbert Stuart portrait of George Washington.

US CAPITOL: Begun in 1793, includes Senate, House of Representatives, Old Supreme Court and statuary hall.

NATIONAL ARCHIVES: The Declaration of Independence and the US Constitution (original documents).

ARLINGTON NATIONAL CEMETERY: The Tomb of the Unknown Soldiers (World Wars I and II); Grave of President John F. Kennedy. The Custis-Lee Mansion, home of Confederate General Robert E. Lee, is also on the grounds.

LINCOLN MEMORIAL: The sculpture by Daniel Chester French is a masterpiece.

JEFFERSON MEMORIAL: Its rotunda follows an architectural form frequently used by him.

SMITHSONIAN INSTITUTION: Among the thousands of historic, scientific and artistic displays are Lindbergh's plane "Spirit of St. Louis," and gowns of all First Ladies of the USA.

MOUNT VERNON: George Washington's home (1754), beautifully preserved.

THE OLD SOUTH

VIRGINIA

RICHMOND: The State Capitol (1785) designed by Jefferson contains Houdon's statue of Washington.

CHARLES CITY: Among the architecturally and historically important James River plantations are Berkeley (1726), family home of William Harrison (ninth President) and Benjamin Harrison (23rd President); Shirley (1769), home of General Robert E. Lee's grandfather; and Westover (1730), home of the Byrd family.

ALEXANDRIA: Christ Church (1773), regularly attended by Washington.

COLONIAL WILLIAMSBURG: The 18th Century capital of Virginia. The Governor's Palace, Capitol, Raleigh Tavern and many other buildings have been reconstructed from the original plans and authentically furnished.

JAMESTOWN: First permanent English settlement in USA (1607). Colonists' ships and fort have been reconstructed.

CHARLOTTESVILLE: Monticello, home of President Thomas Jefferson (1769) shows many of his ingenious inventions in architecture and furniture.

YORKTOWN: Fortifications and exhibits pertaining to last major battle of the Revolutionary War and surrender of British forces of Lord Cornwallis (1781).

NORTH CAROLINA

MANTEO: Fort Raleigh, first English attempt at colonization (1585) has been reconstructed.

WINSTON-SALEM: Old Salem (1766) was a pioneer experiment in communal living by the Moravians.

WILMINGTON: The World War II battleship *USS North Carolina* is preserved as a memorial.

CHEROKEE: Oconaluftee Indian Museum, restoration of 18th Century Indian village.

SOUTH CAROLINA

CHARLESTON: Fort Sumter was bombarded in attack which started the Civil War. Dock Street Theater is the first theater in USA. Charleston has innumerable fine 18th Century buildings.

COLUMBIA: Confederate Museum in State Archives Building. Boyhood home of President Woodrow Wilson.

GEORGETOWN: Early (1735) rice and indigo port. Important sights include Belle Isle Gardens, an early plantation, the Winyah Indigo Society Hall (1857), and the Greek Revival County Court House (1824).

GEORGIA

ATLANTA: The Grant Park cyclorama of Battle of Atlanta (1864) was painted from sketches by eyewitnesses. This is one of the world's largest paintings.

SAVANNAH: Fort Pulaski (National Monument), captured by Union forces in 1862. Factors' Walk, a row of 19th Century cotton warehouses.

WARM SPRINGS: The "Little White House," Georgia home of President Franklin D. Roosevelt.

CHICKAMAUGA and CHATTANOOGA NATIONAL MILITARY PARK: The largest such park in the USA, site of important Civil War battles in 1863.

FLORIDA

PENSACOLA: The Naval Air Station includes a Museum of Naval Aviation as well as Fort San Carlos (1696) and Fort Pickens (1834).

CAPE KENNEDY: The rocket launching center can be seen from a distance and there is a roadside display of missiles.

ST. AUGUSTINE: Castillo de San Marcos (1672), built by the Spaniards over a period of 84 years.

ALABAMA

MONTGOMERY: The First White House of the Confederacy (1852) exhibits mementos of Confederate President Jefferson Davis and his family.

MOBILE: Fort Morgan, active in the War of 1812 and Civil War, is excellently preserved.

BIRMINGHAM: Arlington Historical Shrine is a good example of an ante-bellum home (1842) with antique furniture.

MISSISSIPPI

JACKSON: The Old State Capitol (1839) has been restored as a historic museum; Confederate trenches for the defense of the city survive.

VICKSBURG: The National Military Park preserves many of the defenses of the city in 1863, when its capture gave control of the Mississippi River to Union Forces. Museum. A large sternwheel riverboat (museum) completes the picture.

NATCHEZ: "D'Evereux," exceptionally fine Greek Revival mansion (1840); many other ante-bellum mansions.

LOUISIANA

NEW ORLEANS: The French Quarter, 18th Century French houses with courtyard gardens and iron grillwork balconies; Garden District, area of fine ante-bellum architecture and gardens; Jackson Square, historic center of city with cathedral (1794-1851) and old Spanish Cabildo, or government headquarters (1795). Birthplace of jazz.

OLD RIVER ROAD: Follows the Mississippi from New Orleans to Baton Rouge. Numerous plantation mansions of the first half of 19th Century.

CHALMETTE NATIONAL HISTORICAL PARK: Site of General Andrew Jackson's (later President) victory in War of 1812. Museum.

TENNESSEE

CHATTANOOGA: Chickamauga and Chattanooga National Military Park; Lookout Mountain, site of the Civil War "battle above the clouds".

NASHVILLE: The Hermitage (1835), mansion of President Andrew Jackson.

MEMPHIS: Goyoso Hotel (1844), used as headquarters by both sides in the Civil War. DeSoto Park, site of the discovery of the Mississippi River by the Spanish explorer DeSoto. Beale Street, made famous in the "Blues" of jazz composer W. C. Handy.

ARKANSAS

LITTLE ROCK: Territorial capitol restoration of the Old State House and twelve other important buildings of the town as it was in the 1830s.

FORT SMITH: A starting point for wagon trains during California Gold Rush. The Old Commissary (1839) is a museum of pioneer relics.

EUREKA SPRINGS: The Ozark Museum displays antiques and music boxes, and Miles Mountain Musical Museum contains unusual old musical instruments.

THE EARLY FRONTIERS

KENTUCKY

HARRODSBURG: Reconstruction of Fort Harrod, first permanent US settlement in Kentucky (1774), cabin in which President Lincoln's parents were married, and the Mansion Museum with an excellent collection of guns, are all in Pioneer Memorial State Park.

ASHLAND: The home of the "Traipsin' Woman" is a museum of Kentucky mountain music.

HODGENVILLE: Abraham Lincoln National Historical Park, log cabin in which he is believed to have been born (1809).

WEST VIRGINIA

HAWKS NEST STATE PARK: Cabin Museum of pioneer relics.

CHARLESTON: State Capitol Museum with Daniel Boone's rifle and other pioneer relics.

HARPER'S FERRY: Scene of the John Brown anti-slavery insurrection (1859) and of battles of the War Between the States. Railroad engine house where Brown was captured is now on campus of Storer College.

OHIO

DAYTON: Air Force Museum; 1850 Greek Revival Court House, scene

of Lincoln-Douglas debate for election to the US Senate (1858).

CINCINNATI: Birthplace of President Taft, an 1820 Federal mansion (museum).

ZOAR: This early religious colony contains a garden based on the Bible's description of the New Jerusalem, the "Number One House" (1835) Museum, Meeting House, Village Store and Gardener's House.

ILLINOIS

CAIRO: This town was the "steamboat metropolis" of the Mississippi River; parts remain unchanged from a century ago. "Magnolia Manor" (1869-72) has been furnished as a museum of the "gaslight era."

SPRINGFIELD: Abraham Lincoln's home (1844) and tomb.

NEW SALEM STATE PARK: Restoration of frontier town as it appeared in Lincoln's youth (1830s).

CHICAGO: The Old Water Tower is one of the few buildings to survive Great Fire of 1871.

INDIANA

LAFAYETTE: Tippecanoe Battlefield, where Harrison (later President) battled Indians in 1811; museum of battle mementos and Indian paintings.

NEW HARMONY: Once an experimental Utopian Community (1825), its garden labyrinth and "gothic" laboratory survive.

MITCHELL: Spring Mill State Park has a reconstructed pioneer village of 1830s including a grist mill, sawmill, store, post office and tavern.

MICHIGAN

DETROIT: The Historical Museum features displays concerning the State's early history; Fort Wayne Military Museum (1848) is a restoration; the President Ulysses S. Grant House is one he occupied with his bride in 1849.

CAMBRIDGE JUNCTION: The Walker Tavern (1833) is a stagecoach inn restored with its original furnishings.

DEARBORN: Greenfield Village, vast museum of historic buildings, vehicles, machinery and other mementos of the 19th Century and industrial revolution.

MINNESOTA

GRAND PORTAGE: Explorers' and fur traders trail (1731) from Lake Superior to Pigeon River is still clearly visible.

MENDOTA: First permanent settlement in the State's territorial period (1830s).

PIPESTONE: Pipestone National Monument includes quarries of unusual red stone from which Indians carved ceremonial peace pipes. Numerous Indian exhibits.

WISCONSIN

PRAIRIE DU CHIEN: American Fur Company Warehouse, the Brisbois House, and the "Villa Louis" Mansion (1843) survive from the time when this was an important center of the fur trade.

BARABOO: State Historical Society Museum of circus history.

MILTON: Milton House Inn (1844) of hexagonal shape. Once a station on the "Underground Railroad," route of slaves escaping to freedom.

THE WILDERNESS AND THE WAGONS

IOWA

WEST BRANCH: Birthplace and library of President Herbert Hoover.

COUNCIL BLUFFS: Log-cabin historical and Indian museum in Lincoln Park; Monument commemorating council of explorers Lewis and Clark with Indians in 1804.

DAVENPORT: Fort Armstrong Blockhouse (1816) has been reconstructed. The Public Museum contains a pioneer wagon of 1840 and an important collection of Mound Builder Indian relics.

MISSOURI

HANNIBAL: The Samuel Clemens House Museum (boyhood home of the author Mark Twain).

ST. LOUIS: Old Rock House (1819) once a warehouse of J. J. Astor, pioneer fur trader.

INDEPENDENCE: President Harry S. Truman Library. Extraordinary historic murals of the pioneer trails.

ST. JOSEPH: Stables of Pony Express to California (1860); house of outlaw Jesse James (1882).

KANSAS

ABILENE: Boyhood home of President Eisenhower; military and presidential museum.

LEAVENWORTH: Fort Leavenworth (1827), starting point for pioneer wagons. The museum has a large collection of early vehicles, guns and other frontier relics.

DODGE CITY: Beeson Museum of mid-19th Century pioneer days in this cattlemen's town.

NEBRASKA

CHIMNEY ROCK: Landmark rising 500 feet above the plains on the Oregon Trail (1840s-1880s); also Court House Rock and Jail Rock nearby.

GERING: Scott's Bluff National Monument and museum of the Oregon Trail.

VALENTINE: Fort Niobrara National Wildlife Refuge maintains a museum, and exhibition herds of American bison (buffalo), elk and Texas longhorn cattle.

OKLAHOMA

ANADARKO: Museum of the Southern Plains Indians displays their costumes, weapons, arts and crafts.

TULSA: Thomas Gilcrease Institute of American History and Art; paintings, maps and manuscripts relating to the Old West.

BARTLESVILLE: Woolaroc Ranch and Museum, a fine collection of Western art and Indian relics.

NORTH DAKOTA

MEDORA: Theodore Roosevelt National Memorial Park; landmarks from Roosevelt's ranching days in the 1880s, and De Mores Chateau, a cattleman's mansion.

DEVILS LAKE: The original buildings of Fort Totten survive from the 1870s, and now house a pioneer museum.

BISMARCK: The State Historical Museum and Camp Hancock Museum exhibit Indian relics and mementos of pioneer life.

SOUTH DAKOTA

MOUNT RUSHMORE NATIONAL MEMORIAL: Colossal sculptures of heads of Presidents Washington, Jefferson, Lincoln and Theodore Roosevelt, near Keystone in the Black Hills.

CUSTER: Way Museum, a log cabin of 1875, with mementos of General Custer; large herd of buffalo in nearby Custer State Park.

DEADWOOD: Typical Wild West mining town. Adams Museum includes locomotive of 1879. Graves of Calamity Jane and Wild Bill Hickok, two famous characters of the Wild West.

WYOMING

CODY: Birthplace and museum of frontiersman "Buffalo Bill" Cody.

FORT LARAMIE: Strategic fortress (1849) on the Oregon Trail, restored as a National Historic Site and Museum.

FORT BRIDGER: A fur-trading center and important supply post (1843) for pioneers of the Oregon Trail. Surviving buildings include a barracks, now a museum, and a Pony Express stable.

MONTANA

VIRGINIA CITY: Once the territorial capital and a gold boom town, its assay office, blacksmith shop; saloon and Wells Fargo office have been restored. The Thompson-Hickman Memorial Museum contains souvenirs of boom days of the 1860s.

CROW AGENCY: "Custer's Last Stand" (1876) Battlefield, National Monument, Cemetery and Museum. None of the US forces survived the battle of Little Big Horn, against the Indians of Chief Sitting Bull.

HELENA: Historical dioramas in State Museum. Principal business street runs along Last Chance Gulch, where gold was discovered in 1864.

IDAHO

BOISE: Pioneer Village includes primitive cabins. Halladay Stagecoach Station, the 1872 US gold assay office and elaborate De Lamar Mansion.

POCATELLO: Ross Park contains prehistoric Indian petroglyphs (rock inscriptions); Idaho State College has an interesting historical museum.

SILVER CITY: Once world famous for its gold and silver mines, now a ghost town with a deserted church, courthouse, saloons and hotel.

UTAH

SALT LAKE CITY: Mormon Tabernacle and Temple; Beehive House (1855) residence of Mormon leader, Brigham Young.

WANSHIP: The Overland Stagecoach Station (1862) is one of few that survive.

OGDEN: Cabin of Miles Goodyear, Utah's first US settler (1844). Several houses with multi-family entrances.

WASHINGTON

SACAJAWEA: Historical State Park. Site of Lewis and Clark expedition camp (1805), large display of Indian artifacts.

SEATTLE: Washington State Museum; excellent Northwest Indian collection.

WALLA WALLA: Museum and ruins of the Whitman Mission (1836), blacksmith shop and grist mill. The mission taught agriculture and industry to the Indians.

OREGON

WOLF CREEK: The Tavern (1857) has been operating since stagecoach days and remains much the same.

THE DALLES: Fort Lee (1847) was built to protect pioneers who put their wagons on rafts here to float down the Columbia River. Wasco County Historical Museum of Indian and pioneer mementos.

ASTORIA: Fort Clatsop (1805) restored winter quarters of Lewis and Clark expedition. The USA's first settlement on Pacific Coast.

GOLD AND CATTLE IN THE WEST

TEXAS

SAN ANTONIO: The Alamo, site of the most famous battle for Texan independence (1836). Museum with relics of US frontiersmen Jim Bowie and Davey Crockett.

AUSTIN: Ante-bellum Governor's Mansion open to visitors; Texas Memorial Museum includes historical displays; Daughters of the Confederacy Museum of the War Between the States.

FORT WORTH: Museum of Western Art with many paintings by Frederick Remington and Charles Russell, the most famous painters of Western life.

NEW MEXICO

SANTA FE: Spanish Palace of the Governors (1610-12), outstanding Spanish-Indian architecture, museums of history and Indian arts; Mission of San Miguel (1636); Museum of Navajo ceremonial art.

ACOMA: The cliff-top Indian Pueblo is one of the oldest continuously inhabited communities in USA.

TAOS: The Church of St. Francis of Assisi (1732) is notable for its bold architecture and a beautiful altarpiece. Indians live in centuries-old pueblos nearby.

ARIZONA

NAVAJO NATIONAL MONUMENT: Three impressive cliff-dwellings of the 13th Century.

TOMBSTONE: Famous Wild West mining and cattlemen's town. OK Corral, Boot Hill Cemetery, Crystal Palace Bar and Saloon, Bird Cage Theater, Schieffelin Hall (1881) former "opera house," now a museum.

MONTEZUMA CASTLE NATIONAL MONUMENT: Indian cliff-dwelling occupied from 13th to 15th Centuries.

TUCSON: San Xavier Del Bac, unusually beautiful Spanish Mission (1783); very complete Arizona State Museum of Archaeology; Pioneer Historical Society Museum of frontier period.

NEVADA

VIRGINIA CITY: Colorful mining boom town (1859), site of the Comstock silver deposit. Piper's Opera House where Edwin Booth performed, Crystal Bar, Bucket of Blood Saloon, "The Castle," and the Bowers Mansion. Edwin Booth's brother, John Wilkes Booth, assassinated President Lincoln.

CARSON CITY: Old Mint produced coins from silver of Comstock Lode. Museum of Indian and pioneer relics, and working model of mine.

LAS VEGAS: The ghost towns of Eldorado, Rhyolite and Beatty are nearby.

COLORADO

CENTRAL CITY: Gilpin County Mining and Historical Museum exhibits pioneer relics and a working gold mine. Restored Opera House of 1878. President Grant visited Teller House Hotel built in 1872.

COLORADO SPRINGS: The Territorial Capitol is a log cabin where the first legislature met. The Pioneer Museum contains archaeological and historic exhibits.

CRIPPLE CREEK: This boom town was called "the $300,000,000 cow pasture" in 1859. The Imperial Hotel and the Cripple Creek District Museum preserve the history of the gold mines and camps.

CALIFORNIA

MONTEREY: Spanish capital (1775), stone and adobe Old Custom House, Presidio (military and government headquarters), and Royal Presidio Chapel from Spanish days. First theater in California, (1846).

SAN FRANCISCO: Mission Dolores (1776); Montgomery Block, one of few downtown buildings to survive earthquake of 1906; Wells Fargo Bank Museum.

SANTA BARBARA: Santa Barbara Mission, unusually beautiful and well preserved, in continuous use since 1786.

SACRAMENTO: Sutter's Fort State Historical Monument is a reconstruction of the 1839 settlement and trading post. The gold discovery of

1848 was made at Sutter's Mill, 50 miles to the east.

SAN DIEGO: The first Spanish settlement in California (1769), of which some traces of the Old Town Plaza remain. San Diego de Alcala, the first of the California missions (1769-1774).

NEW FRONTIERS

ALASKA

SITKA: Sitka National Monument exhibits an impressive collection of Haida Indian totem poles. St. Michael's Russian Orthodox Cathedral (1844).

JUNEAU: The Historical Museum includes Eskimo crafts; the depleted mines of the 1880 gold rush are nearby.

HAWAII

HONOLULU (Island of Oahu): Bishop Museum exhibits the regalia of the Hawaiian monarchy and a great collection of Pacificana. The sunken battleship *USS Arizona* is preserved as a memorial to the dead of Pearl Harbor.

KAILUA-KONA (Island of Hawaii): Treasures of Hawaiian royalty are exhibited in Hulinee Palace.

PUERTO RICO

SAN JUAN: The Old San Juan section of the city appears much the same as in Spanish colonial days and is surrounded by elaborate fortifications including the fortress of El Morro (1540).

SAN GERMAN: Porta Coeli Church has excellent collection of antique religious art.

VIRGIN ISLANDS OF THE US

ST. CROIX: Christiansted National Historic Site includes 18th Century fort and Government House built by the Danes, as well as store where Alexander Hamilton, first US Secretary of the Treasury, worked as a young man.

ST. THOMAS: "Bluebeard's Castle" is said to have been a pirate's fort.

ST. JOHN: Many of the 18th Century sugar plantation mansions survive.

For Further Information, Write to . . .

In this section you will find names and addresses, grouped according to kinds of vacations, to whom you can write for information and/or fuller discussions than space allowed in this book.

Sources include the federal government, trade associations, books from various companies, including some publications sponsored by travel-associated companies (e.g., an airline, an oil firm). Also listed are mail-order houses (for catalogs) and companies offering brochures describing the services they sell.

For listings with "Government" as the publisher, you address your request to the Superintendent of Documents, US Government Printing Office, Washington, DC 20402.

Descriptions of the contents of government publications are those supplied by the government.

No addresses are given for publishers who distribute their products through book stores, where you should be able to find the titles listed or have them ordered for you.

For books available only by mail, addresses are furnished.

Listings are alphabetical by category and alphabetical within categories.

CAMPING

American Camping Assn.
14 West 8th St.
New York, NY

American Forestry Assn.
1319 18th St., NW
Washington, DC 20036

Back-Country Travel in the National Park System
A comprehensive guide to more than forty parks that permit travel in back-country areas on foot, on horseback, by canoe and by other means.
Government   35 cents

Backpacking in the National Forest Wilderness, A Family Adventure
Lists equipment needed and procedures to follow for family backpacking. It also lists organizations to contact for further information on the subject.
Government   25 cents

Camping in the National Park System
A guide to camping facilities and accommodations in the National Parks, including camping season, limit of stay, number of sites, fees, food and sanitary services and recreational opportunities.
Government   30 cents

Camping — The National Forests — America's Playgrounds
Lists all the National Forests and tells where to write for information on camping areas in the forests.
Government   25 cents

Continental Auto Camping
Derek Townsend
International Publications
Service $6.25

Enjoy Camping Holidays
Alan Ryalis
International Publications
Service $2.75

Family Camping Federation
Bradford Woods
Martinsville, IN 46151

Guide to European Campgrounds
Rand McNally $4.95

Let's Go Camping: A Guide to Outdoor Living
Harry Zarchy
Knopf $4.49

National Camping & Hiking Assn.
7172 Transit Rd.
Buffalo, NY 14221

National Forest Vacations
Describes the many areas by states that can be visited for camping, sightseeing, fishing, hiking and other outdoor activities and gives an outline of the trails in the National Forests.
Government   55 cents

Search for Solitude
Lists all the wilderness areas in the US administered by the National Forest Service.
Government   65 cents

FARMS AND RANCHES

Arizona
Dept. of Economic Planning & Development
3003 N. Central Av.
Suite 1704,
Phoenix, AZ 85012

Arkansas
Ozark Farm Vacation Assn.
Mrs. Fred Daum, Secretary
Box 3
Pleasant Grove, AR 72567

Farm and Ranch Vacation Guide
Farm and Ranch Vacations, Incorporated
36 East 57th St.
New York, NY 10022 $2.50

Illinois
Farm Vacation & Farm Recreation Areas
222 S. College St.
Springfield, IL 62706

Iowa
Tourism & Travel Div.
250 Jewett Building
Des Moines, IA 50309

Kentucky
Dept. of Agriculture
Div. of Information & Promotion
Capitol Annex
Frankfort, KY 40601

Maryland
Dept. of Agricultural Economics
University of Maryland
College Park, MD 20742

Nebraska
Nebraskaland Ranch-Farm Vacations
Lincoln, NE 68509

New Hampshire
Farm Boarding Houses
State House Annex
Concord, NH 03301

New York
Dude Ranches
State Dept. of Commerce
112 State St.
Albany, NY 12207

Old Butterfield Trail
(wagon trips)
602 A Main St.
Quinter, KS 67752

Oregon
State Highway Dept.
Travel Information Div.
Salem, OR 97310

Outlaw Trails, Inc.
   (Robber's Roost Ranch)
PO Box 336-F
Green River, UT 84525

Pennsylvania
Dept. of Agriculture
Bureau of Markets
2301 N. Cameron St.
Harrisburg, PA 17120

Ranch Kamps of America
PO Box 36
Billings, MT 59103

Vermont
Dept. of Agriculture
Agriculture Building
Montpelier, VT 05602

West Virginia
Travel Development Div.
Charleston, WV 25305

Wisconsin
Dept. of Natural Resources
Box 450
Madison, WI 53701

HIKING

American Pioneer Trails
   Assn.
4828 217th St.
Bayside, NY 11364

American Youth Hostels, Inc.
14 West 8th St.
New York, NY 10014

Appalachian Mountain Club
5 Joy St.
Boston, MA 02108

Audubon Camp
Riversville Rd.
Greenwich, CT 06830

Backpacking
R. C. Rethmel
Burgess $3.75

Backpacking: An Introduction and a Complete Guide
Dick Getzlaff
Nash $7.95

Camping by Backpack and Canoe
Theodore Cheney
Funk & Wagnall $7.95

Complete Walker
Colin Fletcher
Knopf $7.95

Everglades Park Co.
3660 Coral Way
Miami, FL 33145

Federation of Trail &
   Hiking Clubs
1916 Sunderland Place, NW
Washington, DC 36200

First Book of Hiking
C. William Harrison
Watts $3.75

Hikers & Backpackers Handbook
W. K. Merrill
Winchester $5.95

Hiking-Climbing Handbook
Curtis Casewit
Hawthorn $4.95

National Camping &
   Hiking Assn.
7172 Transit Rd.
Buffalo, NY 14221

Sierra Club
1050 Mills Tower
San Francisco, CA 94104

Trailblazer
PO Box 1
Highlands, NC 28741

The Wilderness Society
729 15th St., NW
Washington, DC 20005

Booklet Distributors of
   America
22 West 42nd St.
New York, NY 10036

Castles of the Old World
Robert P. Long
634 Bellmore Av.
East Meadow, NY 11554
$2.50

Holiday Exchange Bureau
PO Box 555
Grants, NM 87020

LLC
18 Rue de Cardinal
   Lemoine 75
Paris 5, France

Overseas Real Estate
1133 Avenue of the
   Americas
New York, NY 10026

Vacation Exchange Club, Inc.
663 Fifth Av.
New York, NY 10022

MAIL-ORDER HOUSES FOR
   OUTDOORS EQUIPMENT

Abercrombie and Fitch
Madison Av. and 45th St.
New York, NY 10017

Phone and mail order:
87-01 69 Av.
Forest Hills, NY 11375

Carikit Outdoor Equipment
PO Box 1153
Boulder, CO 80302

Frostline Outdoor
   Equipment
PO Box 1378 (kits, Box 2190)
Boulder, CO 80302

Herter's
Waseca, MN 56093

L. L. Bean
Freeport, ME 04032

Montgomery Ward & Co.
Write to Montgomery Ward
at one of the following
cities for a mail-order
catalog:
Albany, NY
Baltimore, MD
Chicago, IL

Denver, CO
Fort Worth, TX
Oakland, CA
Portland, OR
St. Paul, MN

Norm Thompson
1815 NW Thurman
Portland, OR 97209

Recreational Equipment
(a co-op, membership $2,
dividends paid yearly)
523 Pike St.
Seattle, WA 98101

Sears Roebuck and Co.
Call your nearest Sears
store to request a mail-
order catalog.

Trailblazer
PO Box 1
Highlands, NC 28741

NATIONAL PARKS,
LANDMARKS, ETC.

*Explore! A Visitor's Guide
to Discovery in the
National Forests*
Lists the Visitor Information
Services of the National Forests.
Government   35 cents

National Parks Pricelist 35
Government   free

National Parks & Landmarks
Lists natural, historical,
recreational and cultural
areas, and National Capital
Parks administered by the
National Park Service, as
well as National Historic,
Natural, and Environmental
Education Landmarks.
Government   75 cents

*States and Territories of the
United States and Their
Resources Pricelist 87*
Government   free

*Winter Activities in the
National Park System*
A guide to downhill and
cross-country skiing, snow-
mobiling, and other winter
sports in the parks, including information on accom-
modations, supplies,

medical assistance, ski
instruction, and winter
access to parks by highway,
bus, train and plane.
Government   35 cents

RECREATIONAL VEHICLE
VACATIONS

*Campground and Trailer
Park Guide*
Rand McNally $4.95

*Campground Guide for
Tent and Trailer Tourists*
Jerry Patterson
Campgrounds Unlimited
Wakefield, KS 67847 $1.95

*Continental Autocamping:
With a Trailer or Motor
Caravan: Buying-Hiring-
Preparing-Holidaying*
Derek Townsend
Fernhill $3.75

Crazy Horse Campgrounds
2152 Dupont Drive
Newport Beach, CA 92664

Cutty's Campgrounds
9th Floor Bank & Trust Bldg.
Des Moines, IA 50309

*Don Parry's Guide to
Northeast Camping Areas*
Outdoor Publishers
PO Box 155
Rocky Hill, CT 06067
$2.00

Holiday Inn Trav-L-Park
3796 Lamar Av.
Memphis, TN 38118

*How to Go Camping and
Motoring Thru Europe*
Paul and Grace Witte
Amity $4.50

Humble Travel Parks
PO Box 2180
Houston, TX 77001

Jellystone Campgrounds, Ltd.
236 Michigan St.
Sturgeon Bay, WI 54235

Kampgrounds of America,
Inc.
PO Box 1138
Billings, MT 59103

King of the Road Tours
120 East Ogden Av.
Hinsdale, IL 60521

*Private Campgrounds,
U.S.A. & Overnight
Trailer Parks with Maps*
Glenn and Dale Rhodes
Box 2652 G
Palos Verdes Peninsula,
CA 90274 $3.95

Ramada Camp Inns
PO Box 590
Phoenix, AZ 85001

Red Arrow Industries
88 Steele
Denver, CO 80206

Safari Camps
Eastgate Plaza
Columbia, MO 65201

*Sportsman on Wheels:
Recreation Vehicles for
Hunters, Fishermen,
Campers and Other
Outdoorsmen*
Irwin Bauer
Dutton $4.50

Stuckey's Camparks
PO Box 370
Eastman, GA 31023

*Sunset Western Campsite
Directory*
Lane Book Co.
Menlo Park, CA 94025
$3.95

*Trailering America's
Highways and Byways —
East and West*
Richard L. Hayes
Trail-R-Club of America
Box 1376
Beverly Hills, CA 90213
$3.95 each volume plus
25 cents handling

*Western Campsites
Directory*
Trailer Coach Assn.
3855 East La Palma Av.
Anaheim, CA 92806

*Wheelers Trailer Resort
and Campground Guides*
Sunbelt, Four Seasons
and *Westerner* editions
G.A. Distributing Company
PO Box 574
Champaign, IL 61820
$2.95 each edition, plus
55 cents handling

*Woodall's Trailering Parks
and Campgrounds*
ed.: Cynthia A. Lockwood
Woodall Publishing Co.
500 Hyacinth Place
Highland Park, IL 60035
$5.95 plus 55 cents handling

TOURS AND GENERAL
TRAVEL
NOTE: Books on travel in
general and on specific
touring information are
legion. This list, necessarily
arbitrary, is the merest
sampling.

Europe on $5 and $10 a Day,
1973-4 editions
Arthur Frommer
Arthur Frommer, Inc.
$3.50

*Fielding's Super Economy
Europe '73*
Nancy Fielding
Fielding Publications, Inc.
$2.95

Fodor's Guide to Europe
ed.: Eugene Fodor
McKay $8.95

*Greece and Yugoslavia on
$5 a Day*
ed.: John Wilcock
Arthur Frommer, Inc.
$2.95

Hawaii on $10 a Day
ed.: Faye Hammel and
Sylvan Levey
Arthur Frommer, Inc.
$2.95

Israel on $10 a Day
Arthur Frommer, Inc.
$2.95

Japan on $10 a Day
John Wilcock
Arthur Frommer, Inc.
$2.95

Mobil Travel Guides
ed.: Marion & Alden Stevens
Simon & Schuster $2.95

New Horizons World Guide
Pan American World
Airways
Simon & Schuster $4.95

WATER TRIPS
Basic Canoeing Textbook
American National Red
Cross   50 cents

*Boating Regulations in the
National Park System*
Federal regulations cover-
ing permits, lifesaving
equipment, commercial
operations, lighting and
signaling devices, and
classifications. Includes
color-coded channel buoy
guide and a guide to the
uniform State Waterway
Marking System.
Government   40 cents

*Fishing in the National
Park System*
Lists fishing opportunities
and regulations in the
National Parks.
Government   30 cents

*Malo's Complete Guide to
Canoeing and Canoe-
Camping*
John Malo
Macmillan $1.95

*North American Canoe
Country*
Calvin Rutstrum
Macmillan $6.95

Foreign Governmental Tourist Offices in the US

The offices listed below are official representatives of foreign
countries. They have tourist literature available and in some cases
they will provide special information on request. They are not travel
agents, make no reservations, sell no tickets.

EUROPE
Austria
Austrian National
Tourist Office
545 Fifth Av.
New York, NY 10017

3440 Wilshire Blvd.
Los Angeles, CA 90005

332 South Michigan Av.
Chicago, IL 60604
Belgium
Belgian Tourist Bureau
589 Fifth Av.
New York, NY 10019

2 South Michigan Av.
Chicago, IL 60603

523 West 6th St.
Los Angeles, CA 90014
Bulgaria
Bulgarian Tourist
Information Office
50 East 42nd St.
New York, NY 10017
Czechoslovakia
Czechoslovak Travel
Bureau
10 East 40th St.
New York, NY 10016

Denmark
Danish National Travel
Office
505 Fifth Av.
New York, NY 10017

209 Post St.
San Francisco, CA 94108

Eire
Irish Tourist Board
590 Fifth Av.
New York, NY 10036

135 South LaSalle St.
Chicago, IL 60603

Finland
Finnish National
Tourist Office
505 Fifth Av.
New York, NY 10017

France
French Government
Tourist Office
610 Fifth Av.
New York, NY 10020

323 Geary St.
San Francisco, CA 94102

Germany
German National
Tourist Office
500 Fifth Av.
New York, NY 10036

11 South LaSalle St.
Chicago, IL 60603

323 Geary St.
San Francisco, CA 94102

Greece
Greek National Tourist
Office
601 Fifth Av.
New York, NY 10017

611 West 6th St.
Los Angeles, CA 90017

Italy
Italian Government
Travel Office
630 Fifth Av.
New York, NY 10020

500 North Michigan Av.
Chicago, IL 60611

St. Francis Hotel
Post St.
San Francisco, CA 94119

Luxembourg
Luxembourg Tourist
Dept.
200 East 42nd St.
New York, NY 10017

Monaco
Monaco Information
Center
610 Fifth Av.
New York, NY 10020

The Netherlands
Netherlands National
Tourist Office
605 Fifth Av.
New York, NY 10017

681 Market St.
San Francisco, CA 94105

Norway
Norwegian Tourist
Travel Office
505 Fifth Av.
New York, NY 10017

Poland
Polish Travel Office
500 Fifth Av.
New York, NY 10036

Portugal
Portuguese Tourist
Information
570 Fifth Av.
New York, NY 10036

Romania
Romanian National
Tourist Office
500 Fifth Av.
New York, NY 10036

Spain
Spanish National
Tourist Office
589 Fifth Av.
New York, NY 10017

180 North Michigan Av.
Chicago, IL 60601

209 Post St.
San Francisco, CA 94102

Sweden
Swedish National
Tourist Office
505 Fifth Av.
New York, NY 10017

612 South Flower St.
Los Angeles, CA 90017

Switzerland
Swiss National Tourist
Office
608 Fifth Av.
New York, NY 10020

104 South Michigan Av.
Chicago, IL 60603

661 Market St.
San Francisco, CA 94105

United Kingdom
British Travel Assn.
680 Fifth Av.
New York, NY 10019

875 North Michigan Av.
Chicago, IL 60611

612 South Flower St.
Los Angeles, CA 90017

USSR
USSR Tourist
Information
45 East 49th St.
New York, NY 10017

Yugoslavia
Yugoslav State Tourist
Office
509 Madison Av.
New York, NY 10022

NORTH AMERICA

Canada
Canadian Government
Travel Bureau
680 Fifth Av.
New York, NY 10019

100 North LaSalle St.
Chicago, IL 60602

510 West 6th St.
Los Angeles, CA 90014

Mexico
Mexican National
Tourist Council
677 Fifth Av.
New York, NY 10022

625 North Michigan Av.
Chicago, IL 60611

9445 Wilshire Blvd.
Los Angeles, CA 90108

BERMUDA, THE BAHAMAS
and THE CARIBBEAN

Antigua
Antigua Tourist Board
20 East 46th St.
New York, NY 10017

Bahama Islands
Bahama Islands Tourist
Office
10 Rockefeller Center
New York, NY 10020

6 North Michigan Av.
Chicago, IL 60602

510 West 6th St. Rm. 516
Los Angeles, CA 90014

Barbados
Barbados Tourist Board
801 Second Av.
New York, NY 10017

Bermuda
Bermuda Tourist &
Trade Development
Board
610 Fifth Av.
New York, NY 10020

6 North Michigan Av.
Chicago, IL 60602

Cayman Islands
Cayman Islands Tourist
Board
51 East 42nd St.
New York, NY 10017

Dominican Republic
Dominican Republic
Tourism
1270 Avenue of
Americas
New York, NY 10020

Haiti
Haiti Government
Tourist Office
30 Rockefeller Plaza
New York, NY 10020

Jamaica
Jamaica Tourist Board
200 Park Av.
New York, NY 10017

36 South Wabash
Chicago, IL 60603

3075 Wilshire Blvd.
Los Angeles, CA 90005

Montserrat
Caribbean Travel
Assn.
20 East 46th St.
New York, NY 10017

Netherlands Antilles
Curacao and Bonaire
Tourist Boards
604 Fifth Av.
New York, NY 10020

Trinidad
Trinidad and Tobago
Tourist Office
Suite 712
400 Lexington Av.
New York, NY 10017

Virgin Islands
Virgin Islands
Government Tourist
Office
16 West 49th St.
New York, NY 10020

CENTRAL AMERICA
Costa Rica
Costa Rican Consulate
General
211 East 43rd St.
New York, NY 10017

6331 Hollywood Blvd.
Los Angeles, CA 90028

Guatemala
Guatemala Tourist
Office
331 Madison Av.
New York, NY 10017

870 Market St.
San Francisco, CA 94102

Honduras
Honduras Consulate
30 East 42nd St.
New York, NY 10017

Nicaragua
Nicaragua Tourist
Information
1270 Avenue of
Americas
New York, NY 10019

Panama
Panama Government
Tourist Bureau
630 Fifth Av.
New York, NY 10020

SOUTH AMERICA
Argentina
Argentina Information
Office
150 SE Second Av.
Miami, FL 33131

Bolivia
Bolivian Consulate
General
10 Rockefeller Center
New York, NY 10020

Brazil
Brazilian Government
Trade Bureau
551 Fifth Av.
New York, NY 10017

Chile
Chilean Consulate
General
809 United Nations
Plaza
New York, NY 10022

Colombia
Colombian Government
Tourist Board
140 East 57th St.
New York, NY 10022

Ecuador
Ecuadorian Consulate
General
1270 Avenue of
Americas
New York, NY 10020

El Salvador
El Salvador Travel
Information
748 Lexington Av.
New York, NY 10022

Peru
Peruvian Consulate
General
10 Rockefeller Plaza
New York, NY 10020

Surinam
Surinam Tourist
Bureau
1 Rockefeller Plaza
New York, NY 10020

Uruguay
Uruguayan Consulate
17 Battery Place
New York, NY 10004

Venezuela
Venezuelan Govern-
ment Tourist Bureau
485 Madison Av.
New York, NY 10022

THE MIDDLE EAST
Cyprus
Cyprus Mission to the UN
165 East 72nd St.
New York, NY 10021

Iran
Iranian Consulate
General
630 Fifth Av.
New York, NY 10020

Iraq
Iraq Tourist Information
14 East 79th St.
New York, NY 10021

Israel
Israel Government
Tourist Office
574 Fifth Av.
New York, NY 10036

5 South Wabash Blvd.
Chicago, IL 60603

8929 Wilshire Blvd.
Beverly Hills, CA 90211

Jordan
Jordan Tourist Infor-
mation Center
866 UN Plaza
New York, NY 10017

Kuwait
Kuwait Consulate
235 East 42nd St.
New York, NY 10017

Lebanon
Lebanon Tourist
Information Office
527 Madison Av.
New York, NY 10022

Syria
Syrian Consular
Service
8 East 66th St.
New York, NY 10021

Turkey
Turkish Information
Service
500 Fifth Av.
New York, NY 10036

AFRICA

Cameroon
Cameroon Mission to
the UN
866 UN Plaza
New York, NY 10017

Congo
Kinshasa Mission to
the UN
400-2 East 51st St.
New York, NY 10022

Dahomey
Dahomey Mission to
the UN
4 East 73rd St.
New York, NY 10021

Egypt
United Arab Republic
Tourist Office
630 Fifth Av.
New York, NY 10020

Ethiopia
Calvert-Stearns, Inc.
157 West 57th St.
New York, NY 10019

Ghana
Ghana Information
Service
Room 516
565 Fifth Av.
New York, NY 10017

Ivory Coast
Ivory Coast Visa Office
521 Fifth Av.
New York, NY 10017

Kenya
Kenya Tourist Office
120 West 57th St.
New York, NY 10019

Libya
Libya Consulate
866 UN Plaza
New York, NY 10017

Morocco
Morocco National
Tourist Office
597 Fifth Av.
New York, NY 10017

Nigeria
Nigerian Mission to
the UN
757 Third Av.
New York, NY 10017

Rhodesia
Rhodesia National
Tourist Bureau
535 Fifth Av.
New York, NY 10017

South Africa
South Africa Tourist
Corp.
610 Fifth Av.
New York, NY 10020

Tanzania
Tanzania Mission to
the UN
205 East 42nd St.
New York, NY 10017

Tunisia
Tunisia Embassy
2408 Massachusetts Av.
Washington, DC 20008

Uganda
Uganda Mission to
the UN
801 Second Av.
New York, NY 10017

Zambia
Zambia National
Tourist Bureau
150 East 58th St.
New York, NY 10022

ASIA

Afghanistan
Afghanistan American
Trading Co.
122 West 30th St.
New York, NY 10001

Burma
Burma Mission to
the UN
10 East 77th St.
New York, NY 10021

Cambodia
Cambodia Mission to
the UN
845 Third Av.
New York, NY 10022

Ceylon
Ceylon Tourist Board
Suite 308
509 Fifth Av.
New York, NY 10017

Hong Kong
Hong Kong Tourist
Assn.
548 Fifth Av.
New York, NY 10036

333 North Michigan Av.
Chicago, IL 60601

617 South Olive St.
Los Angeles, CA 90014

India
Indian Government
Tourist Office
19 East 49th St.
New York, NY 10017

685 Market St.
San Francisco, CA 94105

Indonesia
Indonesian Consulate
General
5 East 65th St.
New York, NY 10022

Japan
Japan National Tourist
Organization
45 Rockefeller Plaza
New York, NY 10020

333 North Michigan Av.
Chicago, IL 60601

727 West 7th St.
Los Angeles, CA 90017

Korea
Korea Tourist Office
48 West 48th St.
New York, NY 10036

Malaysia
Malaysia Dept. of
Tourism
510 West 6th St.
Los Angeles, CA 90014

Nepal
Royal Nepalese
Consulate General
300 East 46th St.
New York, NY 10017

Pakistan
Pakistani Consulate
General
12 East 65th St.
New York, NY 10021

Singapore
Singapore Tourist
Promotion Board
500 Fifth Av.
New York, NY 10036

8 South Michigan Av.
Chicago, IL 60603

251 Post St.
San Francisco, CA 94108

South Vietnam
South Vietnamese
Embassy
2251 R Street
Washington, DC 20008

Thailand
Thailand Tourist
Organization
20 East 82nd St.
New York, NY 10028

510 West 6th St.
Los Angeles, CA 90014

THE PACIFIC

Australia
Australian Tourist
Comm.
630 Fifth Av.
New York, NY 10020

332 South Michigan Av.
Chicago, IL 60604

3600 Wilshire Blvd.
Los Angeles, CA 90005

Fiji Islands
Fiji Islands Visitors
Bureau
3807 Wilshire Blvd.
Los Angeles, CA 90005

New Caledonia
New Caledonia
Tourist Office
6290 Sunset Blvd.
Los Angeles CA 90023

New Zealand
New Zealand
Government Travel
Comm.
630 Fifth Av.
New York, NY 10020

153 Kearny St.
San Francisco, CA 94108

Philippines
Philippines Tourist and
Travel Assn.
15 East 66th St.
New York, NY 10023

Tahiti
Tahiti Tourist Board
501 Madison Av.
New York, NY 10019

6 North Michigan Av.
Chicago, IL 60601

150 Post St.
San Francisco, CA 94108

Taiwan
Chinese Information
Service
100 West 32nd St.
New York, NY 10001

210 Post St.
San Francisco, CA 94108

INDEX

For references pertaining to states, District of Columbia and possessions of the US, see the appendix.

For references pertaining to states, District of Columbia and possessions of the US, see the appendix.

For references pertaining to states, District of Columbia and possessions of the US, see the appendix.

For references pertaining to states, District of Columbia and possessions of the US, see the appendix.